THE
CLIMATE
CHANGE
GARDEN

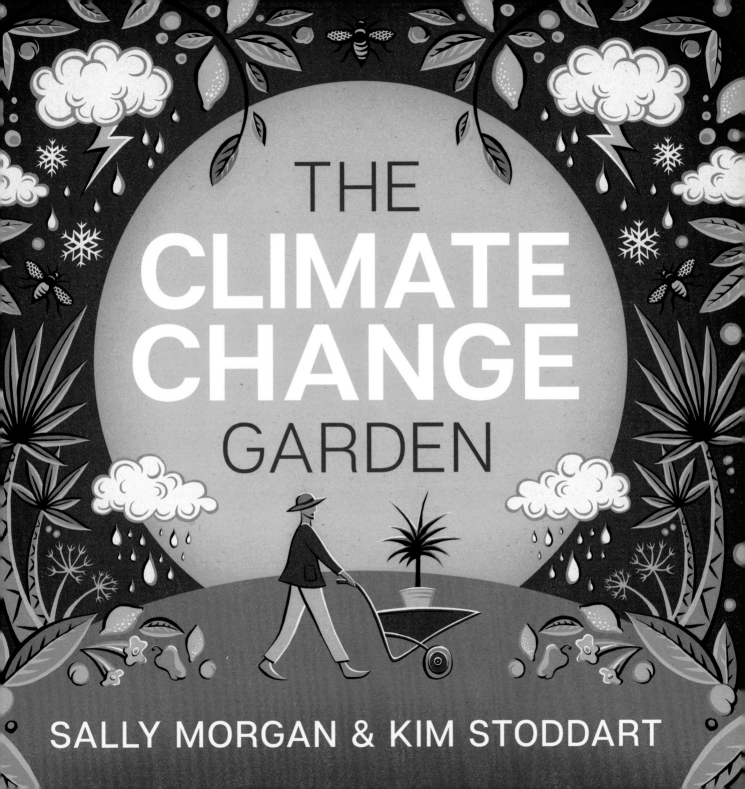

THE
CLIMATE
CHANGE
GARDEN

SALLY MORGAN & KIM STODDART

CONTENTS

FOREWORD

Why it's no longer gardening as usual

The scorching summer of 2018, with its Mediterranean-like high temperatures and many weeks of drought, provided a wake-up call for most citizens of the UK. The long-predicted extremes of weather caused by climate change were well and truly upon us. Actually, they have been for some time, as increasingly wet winters and violent storms have become the new norm for the past few years. Yet it was the recent heatwave that very much 'flicked the switch' on the challenging reality that we now face.

As gardeners, we are often more directly aware of the seasons than many, being tuned to the natural rhythms of germination, growth, fruiting, harvesting, death and renewal of the plants and produce that we tend. We're out in the elements and see first-hand how the weather impacts directly on our gardens. Whilst every year is different, there has always been a comfort to the regular and predictable changing of the seasons; the routines and practices that we have carried out because that is just what we've done at that time of every year.

Yet, there's no getting away from it; the climate and weather patterns of yore are changing fast and our gardening practices need to adapt to catch up. Worldwide, the lack of global leadership on environmental matters continues to frustrate and cause a sense of powerlessness amongst individuals. As gardeners, we already recognise that it's no longer going to be traditional seasons and growing methods, and most of us are extremely worried and looking for answers. Our book aims to provide just that.

After talking about this subject much over the years, in Kim's case in the gardening

Floods may be more frequent

A changing climate may bring more droughts

pages of national publications, such as *The Guardian* and teaching more resilient techniques on her courses, and in Sally's case writing on food, farming and environmental matters, we realised there was a pressing need for an accessible 'how to garden in a changing climate' guide that we, with our respective experience on the subject, could provide.

Of course, the uncertainty of the future we now face is intimidating. Yet, learning how to protect our precious outside space against extreme rain, sunshine, wind, snow and goodness knows what else that is ahead of us, will be key. As will knowing which plants are best placed to deal with such extremities in the first place, the techniques, practices and equipment that can be employed to an existing space, and the future designs that can help to provide a greater robustness. All of this and much more besides is covered in this book, alongside lots of practical take-home advice and inspirational ideas to help you on your way to more resilient gardening.

Kim and Sally
aka the Climate Change Gardeners
(climatechangegarden.uk)

A TASTE OF THINGS TO COME?

Is 2018 going to be typical of the weather to come?

After a very wet winter and late start to spring, with snow on high ground in some parts of the UK in April, our annual planting initially struggled to catch up on growth, and was immediately subjected to a prolonged hot and dry spell. As well as putting further pressure on more delicate planting, gardeners themselves felt the heat stress as they tried desperately to keep up with watering in the seemingly unrelenting rays of sunshine and lack of rain for nigh on two months. Then, just as reservoirs were running dry and hose pipes about to be banned, heavy thunderstorms brought torrential rain and strong winds to the country, breaking the drought. But the weird weather didn't stop at this. There followed an unseasonably warm autumn with trees holding their leaves until November…

Comparatively speaking, when you consider what was happening in other parts of the world, we got off lightly in the UK. Across Europe, there were droughts and forest fires. The Arctic Circle experienced summer temperatures that rose above 30°C (86°F) while California, in the midst of a vicious drought, experienced devastating, wind-driven forest fires that burnt whole towns to the ground. On the other side of the continent, Florida and neighbouring states experienced a series of tropical mega-storms that rolled in from the Atlantic. Further afield, record

Reservoirs dried up in parts of the UK in 2018

Forest fires raged across California in 2018

monsoon floods hit South Asia while parts of Australia experienced the worst drought in living memory.

In the UK, 2018 was the joint hottest on record, despite below average temperatures for March, which was followed by the sunniest May on record. However, this was not the only topsy-turvy year. So was 2012, which started off with a drought and hosepipe bans, but ended as the wettest year ever in England.

What do we know?

The global rise in the levels of carbon dioxide is well documented; it's been happening since the start of the Industrial Revolution, when we started to burn coal. Our addiction to fossil fuels, coupled with deforestation, changes in land use and farming, has boosted the levels of carbon dioxide in the atmosphere from 280 ppm in 1750 to 405ppm in 2018, the highest recorded level for 800,000 years. The current rate of increase is four times that of the 1960s. Carbon dioxide, together with water vapour, methane, ozone, CFCs, and nitrous oxides are called greenhouse gases (GHG) because they trap heat in the atmosphere and cause temperatures to rise, just like a closed greenhouse on a hot day, and it is GHGs that are behind global warming.

Already, human activities have caused the average surface temperature of the planet to increase by about 1°C (1.8°F) above pre-industrial levels, with most of that warming happening between 2006 and 2015. If we don't curb our activities, the surface temperature is predicted to increase by a further 1.5°C (2.7°F) between 2030 and 2052. Different parts of the globe are experiencing more warming than others. For example, it happens more over land than water and it's up to three times greater in the Arctic.

Between 1998 and 2010, the rises in average surface temperatures were not as high as predicted because weather systems and events, such as volcanic eruptions throwing clouds of small particles into the atmosphere and the cooling effect of El Niñas (see page 18), helped to offset human-made changes. But now scientists warn of the opposite and predict a peak warming phase.

Action is needed, and fast, but the trouble is, it's now difficult to stop these changes. We can only hope to slow them down.

What is likely to happen weatherwise?

More heatwaves in Europe, more fires in the US and more droughts in Australia and South Africa are predicted. As the oceans warm up more quickly than the air above them, more energy is picked up by the oceanic weather systems, causing more hurricanes and typhoons and, as a result, more flooding. Professor James Renwick of the Victoria University of Wellington said: "If the warming trend caused by greenhouse gas emissions continues, years like 2018 will be the norm in the 2040s and would be classed as cold by the end of the century." A recent *State of the Climate Report* did not make for comfortable bedtime reading. Written by 500 scientists, the report recorded 2017 as a year that saw sea ice retreating, record high seas, shrinking glaciers, below

Will we see more residential flooding?

average polar ice extent, and the most destructive coral bleaching ever seen. It was the third warmest year on record behind 2016 and 2015, with many countries reporting record-breaking annual temperatures, with higher temperatures being reported further south and north than ever before. There was extreme flooding in Venezuela, Nigeria and South Asia too. Yet more evidence of global warming comes from a new global forecasting system (*Nature Communications*, August 2018) which predicts the world will see more extreme temperatures in the next four years as natural warming reinforces man-made climate change, with no respite until at least 2022, and maybe not even then.

So what does this mean for UK gardeners?

Today, the UK is warmer by an average of about 0.8°C (1.5°F) compared with the period 1961–1990. Obviously, nobody knows how climate change will play out, but experts believe a number of changes will take place. Extremely warm summers are expected to occur more frequently, maybe as much as twice a decade, compared with twice in every 100 years in the early 2000s. By 2040, severe heatwaves may occur every other year. The higher-than-average temperatures will mean a longer growing season.

An increase in average temperature of just 1°C (1.8°F) will extend the growing season by three weeks in the south of England and by 10 days in the north west. There will be longer periods of high temperatures, more tropical nights and milder winters. Northern England is going to be milder too, but is also likely to be wetter in winter and feature more storms.

If temperatures were to rise by 2°C (3.6°F), southern England would experience a climate more like southern France, while a massive 4°C (7.2°F) rise would create a

Learning from the past

Past changes

Climate change is not new. The UK has had periods of warmer weather before. The Romans used to grow grapes and lentils in Britain, and there was a further warm period about 1,000 years ago in Medieval Britain, meanwhile the Little Ice Age (16th to 19th centuries) was a time of cooling and extreme winter weather, with snow on the ground for many months, frequent storms and cold summers. It was cold enough for rivers to freeze over, and to be used for Frost Fairs. The growing season was shorter, crops failed and famine was common. Gardeners adopted the idea of the walled garden to create a microclimate that suited growing vegetables.

climate like that of South West Portugal. By the year 2050, much of the UK will suffer from significant water shortages.

We are already experiencing substantial warming in summer and autumn with the upper temperatures increasing faster than the minimum temperatures, making it more likely that we will experience hot summers. The opposite is happening in winter. Minimum temperatures are

A gravel rockery in Kim's climate change garden

going to be a lot of variation too, with some regions seeing more drought, but other areas becoming wetter in summer. The pattern of rain may change too. It's less likely to fall all year round as it tends to do at the moment. Instead, it's more is likely to fall in winter with weeks of summer drought becoming increasingly common. There will be intense down-pours and a greater likelihood of flash floods. Flooding is going to be one of the biggest challenges facing the UK. The sea level around our coasts is already up by about 16cm (6") since 1900 and is pre-dicted to be 40cm to 100cm (1'4" and 3'3") higher by 2100.

We may have warm, dry summers, but winters could be mild and wet and we have to be prepared for more erratic weather – more storms, winds, droughts, extreme high or low temperatures.

Extreme weather gardening

In an established garden, it's not that the weather is too cold or too warm, or that spring is early or frost comes late, that is the problem. It's the fact that all these increasing extreme-weather-variables are tending to occur within a short space of time and garden plants can't cope. It takes

increasing faster than the highest winter temperatures, which means fewer frosts. In fact, by 2040 a frost may be quite rare in South West England and, looking well ahead to 2080, a frost may be a one-in-10 year event. Snowfall, too, will be less common, even in the highlands of Scot-land. That really will alter our growing patterns.

A warmer climate, though, doesn't mean a drier climate. Over the last few decades, rainfall has actually increased in some places, especially in Scotland. There's

Kim's naturalistic gardens work with nature, rather than trying to meticulously control it.

Will our lawns weather out the climate change storm?

THE **CLIMATE CHANGE** GARDEN

a resilient plant to survive all that nature throws at it, and in a climate-changed world, it's not just the long-term rise in temperatures, but the extreme weather events that make it so disrupting for plants. These stresses makes them more vulnerable to pests and disease.

It's no longer gardening as usual

We're already seeing changes – the earliest spring, the mildest winter, the wettest year. New pests and diseases are being reported every year. Gardens take years to mature, so if our gardens in 10, 20, 30, even 80 years ahead have any chance of surviving the future climate, we need to start implementing plans for change right now.

Urban gardens are likely to be leading the change as towns and cities will see greater shifts in weather patterns due to the 'heat island' effect caused by the presence of streets, buildings and traffic, which all generate heat. There will be new challenges too, such as coping with heavy downpours that create flash floods and waterlogging.

It's going to be hard and as gardeners, we are going to have to make uncomfortable changes and maybe lose some of our best-loved features. Which of our favourite garden trees will be able to survive the buffeting of storms or the stress of drought? Will you even want a lawn? Will the classic cottage garden survive? What about our rose gardens? Head gardeners in charge of major gardens are already adapting and planning for the future, so you should too.

Yet it's not all doom and gloom as the changes offer opportunities too. No more mowing the lawn if gravel gardens take pride of place instead, and exotic tropical plants may fill the flower borders. You may lose a few favourites but gain new ones – how about growing aubergines, chickpeas, soybeans and lentils in the veg plots and palms in the flower beds?

You will need to listen to your garden – pay attention to what is happening now, learn from hard lessons and try to work out how to best cope with the many changes that are to come. How are you going to adapt your garden to climate change? HRH The Prince of Wales was reported as saying that he is planting trees for his grandchildren to enjoy. That's a lovely sentiment, but what species should he be planting? What should you be planning for in your garden for 10, 20, and even 30 years ahead?

What causes unusual weather patterns?

Weird weather patterns are often linked to solar activity. European weather is very dependent on the jet stream. This is a jet of warm air that blows from west to east, across the Atlantic, giving North West Europe its mild climate. But a period of low solar activity throws the jet stream off its normal pattern. It may shift north or south of its usual route and cause what meteorologists call a Sudden Stratospheric Warming (SSW). It was this type of shift in the jet stream that caused the big freeze of 2010 and 'The Beast from the East', which blanketed parts of the country in snow in 2018.

Other important weather factors are El Niño and El Niña years. These are regular shifts in patterns of weather in the eastern tropical Pacific Ocean that occur every few years and have effects that are felt throughout the world. The 2015 El Niño effect was one of the strongest ever seen, with massive ocean warming. The effect usually lasts for about a year and it warms up the surface of the Pacific and weakens the trade winds, causing changes in wind patterns and rainfall. The extra energy from the warmer ocean heats up the atmosphere which creates more intense weather events. This leads to increased rainfall in

South and North America with below-average temperatures.

El Niña is the opposite, as the ocean waters of the eastern Pacific are cooler and the trade winds are stronger. This can even lead to an increased risk of colder winters in the UK.

Record-breaking years

1962–63: The Big Freeze One of the coldest winters on record, with lakes and rivers freezing over, and (in Central England) temperatures falling as low as they were in 1659 and 1683 when Frost Fairs took place on frozen rivers. Over New Year, blizzards delivered 6m (20') of snow over the South West and Wales, blocking roads and railways and cutting off villages. The deep snow cover lasted for several weeks. In January, the sea froze for a mile out from the shore at Herne Bay, Kent, and in February, more blizzards extended the misery before the temperature finally rose above freezing in March. Gardens really suffered, as it was too cold for even the most reliable hardy plants.

1976: Heatwave and drought There were 15 consecutive days in mid-summer when the temperatures exceeded 32°C (90°F) somewhere in England. On the hottest day, 3 July, the temperature reached 35.9°C (96.6°F). The problem was made worse by the fact that the preceeding year was dry, so water reserves were already low. The drought ended in late August with severe thunderstorms.

1987: The Great Storm Strong winds felled swathes of mature forest, causing the loss of millions of trees across England and more storms followed in 1990, damaging yet more trees.

2000/2001: Flooding Prolonged rain caused serious flooding and loss of plants due to water-logging. The wettest ever three consecutive months were October to December 2000, with 512.3mm (20.17") of rain

2003: Heatwave The hottest year in Europe on record since 1540 and the UK saw temperatures reach 38.5°C (101.3°F) in Kent. France was particularly hard hit with almost 15,000 heat-related deaths.

2012: Year of floods The year started with a winter drought followed by a heat wave in March. The weather suddenly turned wet and stayed that way for the next year. April was the wettest in 100 years, while early June was the wettest in 150 years. There were thunderstorms in June and July, and a series of intense storms causing widespread flooding and wind damage in September, November, December and January.

2013 to 2015: Storms and flooding The year 2013 started with a coastal surge and record sea levels on north and east coasts, followed by 12 storms in succession and the wettest winter for 250 years, with 11,000 homes flooded. December 2015 was the wettest month ever recorded with 17,000 homes flooded.

2018: Joint hottest on record for the UK and the hottest ever summer for England.

CHAPTER
ONE

TOO MUCH WATER

Does your garden cope well with a heavy and prolonged deluge of rain? When people think of climate change, they anticipate hotter summers and potential water shortages but, perhaps surprisingly, a distinct excess of water will be one of the main problems in the garden in our climate-changed future, alongside coping with summer drought. And there will be more rain during the winter too. If you've experienced flooded beds and a sodden lawn recently – it's really time to get prepared.

Throughout this chapter we'll keep coming back to the basic principles used by landscape architects and permaculturalists – **slow it, spread it and sink it.** In other words, slow down the movement of water, allow it to spread out and create opportunities for the water to drain into the soil where it will be stored for future use. Any excess water that cannot be held by the soil can then be collected in ponds and tanks.

We're expecting more rain

Rainfall records for the UK show that, in the more northern regions, especially the upland areas of Scotland and North of England, rainfall has increased over the last 110 years. The UK has experienced seven out of the 10 wettest years on record since 1998. The winter months from December 2013 to February 2014 were the soggiest in England and Wales since 1766, with around 435mm (17") of rain.

Left: Flooded vegetables in a walled garden

Flood waters around raised vegetable beds in winter

Summer rainfall patterns are changing too, with experts predicting less gentle rain and more heavy monsoon-like downpours.

An estimated five million homes in the UK are at risk of flooding from rivers, coastal or surface waters. With more rain on the cards, combined with the predicted rise in sea levels, flooding is going to become even more commonplace.

Going with the flow

Part of the problem comes from the fact that water levels can rise very quickly. After heavy rain, a trickle in a stream soon becomes a torrent and can flood nearby gardens. Even quite small changes can lead to flooding, such as a blocked drain or culvert. Extensions to buildings, new walls and garages can cause problems as well. For example, a new wall can block the route that water used to take, so

Did you know?

A lot of water falls on a roof in a year. You can calculate just how much by multiplying the annual rainfall (mm) by the roof surface area (m^2) to find the volume in litres that will run off the roof. The average rainfall for the UK is 885 mm. For $100m^2$ of roof that's a massive 88,500 litres of water a year. (For imperial measurements, multiple the square footage of the roof by 0.56 to calculate the number of gallons per inch of rain and then multiply by the annual rainfall in inches.)

after a heavy deluge, water has nowhere to go and floods the ground in front of the wall. Your garden may simply be lower than neigh-bouring gardens, the road, or located at the bottom of a hill, so water flows in. Unless your neighbours install drainage and divert the water running off their garden into yours, you

are going to have problems. But, in the future, your garden may flood after heavy rain simply because it, or the surrounding area can't cope with the volume of water.

Flood warnings – when your garden is at severe risk

It has been raining heavily for a week and you are sent an alert that your home lies in an area that is expected to severely flood. What can you do? Local authorities may distribute sandbags around at-risk areas, but if you live in a water-vulnerable location it may be wise to have your own stockpile of sandbags and flood boards to hand. You can use them to protect areas such as the base of a greenhouse and its glass panels, or to direct water away from a weak wall. Flood boards can also be positioned across a gate to prevent flood water entering a garden.

- move pots and garden ornaments onto walls or higher ground
- secure or weigh down fruit cages, cold frames, chairs and play equipment
- place netting over any pond and secure it tightly, so your fish are not washed away
- weigh down manhole covers with sand-bags to prevent them lifting during flooding and creating a trip risk
- harvest any crops in the ground.

If you are unlucky and your garden is severely flooded, don't forget to take photos for your insurance claim and don't throw anything away until the insurance assessor has visited.

Clearing up

A garden can look a complete mess after surging floodwaters have passed through. It wouldn't be so bad if it was just river water, but most flood water carries with it all sorts of contaminants, including plastic and other waste, sewage, manure, slurry plus chemicals, such as oil, pesticides, and more besides. So, if you suspect that the water is contaminated, wear protective clothing and waterproof boots while in the garden and keep pets away.

It's best to avoid going into the garden until the flood waters have drained away. Before you do so, make sure the electricity supplying any outside sockets is turned off and don't turn it back on until everything has been

If you have time, you can also prepare by doing the following:

- lift pots, bags of compost and equipment off the floor of the greenhouse and shed
- move valuable equipment, such as a lawn mower, onto pallets
- unplug electrical equipment, such as heaters, lights and pond pumps
- turn off the water supply to your garden
- make sure containers of fuel, oil and pesticides etc. are placed on shelves out of reach of any flood waters and that gas cylinder valves are turned off

Quick replacement vegetable beds

If your vegetable plot has been flooded and you have lost your crops, the quickest way to recover is to build some new raised beds and fill them with bought-in compost so that you can still make use of the growing space. The ultimate 'quick fix' raised bed is a one tonne bulk bag filled with compost. You can also make use of containers and grow bags too. But, don't be tempted to fill the new beds with compost from any compost bins that have been flooded.

checked. All the rubbish from a flooded garden is classed as controlled waste as it may be contaminated, so it must be thrown away in skips provided by the local council.

Although it may be tempting to keep sandbags for another time, they should also be thrown away as they will be contaminated. The same is true for any bags of compost, sand from play areas, bark chippings and so on that came into contact with flood water. Never, ever, eat any vegetables that were in the ground at the time of flooding, even those that would normally be cooked. Guidance suggests that the ground should not be used for at least one year and even longer for salad crops, to ensure that sure any contaminants, spores, or disease-causing bacteria are long gone.

Water can also do a surprising amount of damage to the foundations of buildings and retaining walls, so check for damage. Unblock drains and hose down hard surfaces, such as patios, paths and walls. Then check for any cracks or other signs of damage. Don't forget that wooden arches and pergolas may be damaged at ground level.

The soil is going to be waterlogged for some time and, when it is in this state, it is easily damaged and susceptible to compaction, so don't walk on it and cause further harm. If you need to gain access or cross a flower bed, use a scaffold board to spread your weight. And don't forget that lawns, too, will be waterlogged, so don't be tempted to walk on them.

After the flood

If it's a flash flood, it's less likely that long-term damage will have been done, but heavy rain or flood water pouring in from rivers may result in standing water in your garden for days, or even weeks. The excess water drains slowly into the soil and creates waterlogged conditions which can stress plants, but in a different way from heat. The water fills the air spaces in the soil, pushing out the air and creating anaerobic conditions around the roots, which can cause them to die. Few species can cope with waterlogged roots for long, apart from those adapted to living in boggy areas, such as willow.

In the weeks following a flood, look for signs that flooding has damaged your plants; you may notice stunted growth, yellowing of leaves and leaf drop. Leaves wilt because the roots are dying and starting to rot. If you dig up the plant, you will probably see blackened roots and they may smell or have rotted away already. The dying roots mean there is no transpiration stream, so water and nutrients are not moved around the plant and the leaves wilt. It may seem odd that the plant is water-hungry when it's surrounded by water, but in such circumstances the plant has no means of taking it up. You may also notice that bark starts to peel on shrubs and trees, and growth in spring is slow or stunted and some branches start to die back. Prolonged waterlogging may result in the decay of the root systems of herbaceous plants,

so they don't reappear in spring and bulbs may simply rot in the ground. A standing flood in summer will have more serious consequences than a winter one, as the plants will be at their most active and are therefore less able to cope with the flood water.

Helping your plants

Firstly, cut away any dead stems and branches, and prune damaged plants into shape. Once you see some new growth, give the plant an organic feed. Any valuable plants can be gently removed from the ground and their roots washed. Then replant them in a drier part of the garden or a large pot. If you have a lot of plants to rescue, but you still have a waterlogged garden, find the driest area, dig a trench and backfill it with a free-draining mix of soil, grit and compost and use it as a nursery bed while you sort out the rest of the garden out. For plants that are too large to move, dig a shallow trench around them to help the water drain away from their crown. Forking the ground around shrubs and trees helps to boost drainage too.

Flood waters may have carried away some of the soil's nutrients, especially soluble nitrogen, so to repair the damage, mulch your beds with a good compost to boost nutrient and organic matter levels and, if necessary, feed the plants in spring. A long-term slow release organic feed can help trees and shrubs. Don't forget that plants that have damaged roots are

TIP

A really simple, but effective, idea to trap and slow down water is for everybody in the street to simply put a load of buckets on their deck or patio to catch water. They can then empty them gradually after the rain has stopped or use them to refill water butts.

also going to be more susceptible to drought, so they will need plenty of water during dry spells. Damp conditions can persist for some time, so expect more slugs and snails, and fungal disease. Eventually, once the soil is dry, you can start remedial action to get rid of any compaction, for example by forking and loosening the soil.

If there is little you can do to avoid flooding, aim to grow plants that can cope with floods and waterlogged soil (see the Appendix). If you have vegetable beds, avoid growing crops over winter. Instead, focus on planting out in spring and harvest them by late autumn to avoid the wettest months of the year. During the rest of the year, keep the soil covered to protect it and prevent weeds growing, either

Work together

It's surprising just how much difference a group of neighbours can make when it comes to reducing the risk of flood, so where you can, work together. Joint actions might include collecting rainwater by using water butts, avoiding bare dug-over patches of soil (which don't hold water as well), directing water away from a neighbour's garden, and using some of the options described later to slow down the movement of water and reduce the volume leaving one garden and entering that of a neighbour.

with a layer of compost, black plastic, or mulch. And in the long-term, look at some of the slow water options described later, such as building raised beds so that the water runs between the beds, keeping the root zone above the water. Lawns don't thrive with regular flooding and waterlogging, so it may be best to replace a lawn with gravel or decking. You could even plant a bog garden with a raised boardwalk to provide interest and a different vantage point.

Preparing for heavy rain

In a natural ecosystem, most of the rainwater soaks into the ground. While some is taken up by plant roots, most continues downward to the water table. The water is filtered through the rocks, so clean water recharges the water table. However, in gardens, hard landscaping and other impermeable surfaces mean that the water cannot soak into the ground and it has to flow elsewhere.

So... to stop your garden from flooding you need to slow down the movement of water, giving it the chance to soak into the ground or flow gently into local water courses.

The best planning involves observation and therefore, on a day when the rain is thundering down, put on your waterproofs and brave the outside to watch and see first hand how water moves through your garden. This will give you the best insight possible. Check the following:

Observe your garden during torrential rain

- Where does the water run? Does it follow paths and drives or run across beds and lawns?
- Does water pour in from the street or a neighbouring garden?
- Does the water run away or collect?
- Are there any gushing downpipes?
- Are there structures in the garden, such as summerhouses and sheds, that are at risk from flooding and need to be moved?
- And don't forget to look beyond your own plot
- You may be at greater risk of parts of your garden flooding during heavy downpours if you have a sloping outside space. Does your garden slope towards the house or away? What are the lowest points in your garden? Does water collect there?
- Are there any local water courses? Is your garden at the lowest point in the area? If

so, it's more likely that flood water from these streams and ditches will flood your garden rather than that of your neighbours

Armed with this knowledge, you will be able to plan more effectively and don't forget that you may need to involve your neighbours to help shore up your local flood defences.

Slowing down water

Slowing water means encouraging it to move into the soil and reduce runoff. Thankfully, there are lots of ways you can improve the flood resilience of your garden by incorporating clever slow-water features. Here are some to think about:

Mulching Before you start redesigning your garden, think again about your soil. It's such an important natural ally. Spreading a thick layer of compost over the soil each year will boost soil organic matter and create a permeable surface that water can penetrate and drain through (see Chapter 4). Bare soil, devoid of mulch or plant, won't be able to absorb much rainfall and it will be more susceptible to nutrient leaching during the winter so, whatever you do, don't leave it uncovered. Instead, mulch it with compost, cover it with plastic or grow a green manure. Trees are useful, too, as their roots absorb water from over a large area, so a garden with trees and shrubs can absorb more water than the same area of outside space without such planting.

TIP

Trees are susceptible to flooding and standing water, so new trees can be planted on gentle mounds, to help water run away from the trunk and roots.

Raised beds can be incredibly useful in gardens where water collects. In fact, some permaculture gardens flood the land deliberately to bring in nutrients, letting the water run between the raised beds (rather like a traditional water meadow that is flooded in winter). The advantage of a raised bed is that it lies above the water level, so the soil does not get waterlogged. You can read more about this in Chapter 5.

Avoiding large areas of concrete and other impermeable surfaces is important as they create a lot of run off. Instead, use paving stones, bricks or gravel so that water can seep through the gaps. If you do need an area of hard standing, think about a porous asphalt or permeable concrete so some of the water can soak in rather than run off.

The gravel paths and raised beds help to make this garden flood-resilient

French drains and weeping tiles A French drain is a small trench that is backfilled with gravel. It allows water to drain away from a building, driveway or lawn, stopping water from collecting and reducing the risk of flash floods. To improve the flow of water further, a perforated drainage pipe known as a weeping tile is laid along the bottom of the trench to help carry water away from the house to an area that can cope with the water or to a soakaway. Weeping tiles were once made from terracotta, but nowadays they are plastic.

Soakaways It is usual practice for house downpipes to direct water along French drains into a soakaway to allow it to sink into the ground. Builders use a formula to calculate how much water will be pouring off the roof and design the size and length accordingly. A soakaway is usually at least 5m (16') from the house so that water does not drain back towards the foundations. It's typically about 1m (3'3") wide and 1.5m deep (4'11"), backfilled with gravel and positioned so that it is found in the lowest part of the garden where

Drains help to carry water away from the lawn

A pebble-lined drainage channel

water can flow in and drain away. However, soakaways don't work on heavy clay soil as the water cannot flow easily through the clay. Any garden structure with a roof, such as a shed or garage, may simply drain on to the ground, so you may need to improve drainage nearby by installing French drains and a small soakaway. Water from downpipes should not enter the sewers, in case overloading them creates an overflow. If you have downpipes, don't let them discharge near the building, but extend them so they direct the water further away towards grass or flower beds where the water has a chance to permeate into the ground.

Water butts and storage tanks are great for harvesting water for use in the garden in summer but, once they are full in winter, they are no help at all in slowing down the impact of heavy rainfall. After a storm, when they are full to capacity, it is best to let the water drain away gradually so that, when it rains again, they can collect a large volume of water. Remember to make sure the valves are closed from April onwards so you have plenty of water for summer.

Another option to consider is the use of leaky barrels filled with gravel. The run off from the roof collects in the barrel, but only drains out slowly. This is called attenuation. While water butts and tanks help to intercept water pouring off roofs, you need to connect them to a system of drains, so the water is moved to places where it can slowly flow away.

A downpipe empties into a drain and soakaway

A swale carries away excess water

Swales and berms Slopes are vulnerable areas in the garden and it's vital to avoid areas of bare ground. Water moves down a slope at speed, taking the shortest route and can carry soil with it, causing soil erosion. You may think that soil erosion only occurs on farmland or cleared forest land, but it can happen in your garden too. It's a good idea to try to reduce the slope by terracing and use swales to carry the excess water away. Swales are ditches that are built along the garden contours and are physical barriers to slow down the movement of water and runoff. The raised bank beside the swale is called a berm and they work together to slow run off, with the swale filling with water and slowing down its movement. Swales can be built so that they direct water to a soakaway, a rain garden or a storm drain (see Chapter 5).

Permeable paths Paths can inadvertently become routes for water to rush through the garden and collect in one area. To avoid this, make sure the path has a permeable surface rather than a hard one or follows a more sinuous route, following contours, so the flow of water is slowed down by forcing it to take a longer path. Another point to watch is that, with more rain in winter, paths are more likely to be damp and covered with algae and moss.

Right: A permeable gravel path

Clever design directs water away from the path

A green roof holds water and releases it slowly

Sump pit If you still get water collecting in your garden, you can build a sump pit at the lowest point. A sump is ideally a one-metre-square, or one-yard-square, area dug as deep as necessary to let the water drain away. It is often simply backfilled with hardcore, such as old bricks and stones, but a modern technique is to use plastic 'attenuation crates' surrounded by a permeable membrane. The sump is topped with a final layer of gravel. It collects water that has been directed through drainage trenches away from the house.

Green roofs and vertical gardens Covering surfaces with vegetation will help to absorb some of the water and reduce the flow through the downpipes. Nowadays, green roofs are quite common and are generally planted with sedum and other succulents that are tolerant of the drought conditions that can exist in the summer months, or with turf (see page 92).

Rain gardens A rain garden is simply a shallow depression, backfilled with a well-drained soil and filled with plants that can cope with being flooded on a temporary basis. Rain gardens are great at temporarily holding storm water, slowing down water run-off from hard surfaces and, as a bonus, they act as a natural filter. The best place to build your rain garden is several metres away from the house on a flat area or one with only a gentle slope (< 10°). Swales and downpipes direct the water away from the house to the rain garden where it collects and from there drains into the ground or is directed by an overspill area or weeping tile to another area of the garden. For obvious reasons, a rain garden needs to be located well away from septic tanks and wells. For more details see page 89.

CASE STUDY

KIM'S FLOODED GARDEN

It was the winter after the steeply inclined grass field at the back of my plot had been ploughed over, that my gardens flooded. The influx of water was so fast and prolonged that for days my veg patch sat under inches of water, the soil was waterlogged and the crops rotted. The damage caused in such a short space of time was immense and, for me, it was a wake-up call. I needed to shore up my gardening defences and fast!

I understood how it had happened because I written previously about soil and its structure with regards to climate change resilience. Once my neighbour's land had been turned over, its ability to absorb and retain water became greatly diminished almost overnight and this was the devastating, gushing result.

To compensate, I created a swale and berm along the back of my garden, with a planting of trees, soft fruits and fast-growing willow to help absorb some of the excess moisture. Allowing the grass to grow long also helped to slow the flow, as did the addition of raised beds, interlinked with permeable gravel pathways. These pathways now allow me to walk

on the ground without causing damage as the water slowly seeps away. Additionally, the use of much longer-lasting perennial plants and winter ground cover on the vegetable patch provide greater protection against the risk of valuable nutrients leaching out of my soil.

These measures, combined with the vital addition of well-composted loam, means my gardens are now able to absorb (and stand firm) against a much greater volume of water than they would have been able to previously.

CHAPTER TWO

HEAT AND DROUGHT

Originally, when we first heard about climate change, it was in terms of more Mediterranean-like summers for the UK. It was easy to imagine hot, balmy evenings and the rather exciting potential of growing a wider range of exotic produce outside, while participating in lots of enjoyable alfresco dining on our home-grown fare. People even joked at the time about how good climate change sounded. Many were actively-looking forward to the prospect of this wonderful Mediterranean lifestyle. Yet, the reality isn't as clear cut by any means.

As we've already explored, the climatic changes and overall temperature rise will indeed herald more heatwaves, just that they will do so alongside more extreme weather patterns in general. So, the picture we were painted was just a rose-tinted snapshot, if you will, of the weather that we now face.

It's probably no surprise, given the scientific projection, that it was the scorching summer of 2018 that suddenly brought into focus the reality that change is indeed upon us. The many winter storms and floods obviously didn't fit into this cosy, ingrained image of what global warming is actually about.

About the cyclical natural phenomena

A study in *Nature Communications* in 2018, outlining the predictions of a new global forecasting system, suggests we are likely to see a boosting of extreme temperatures in the next four years at least. And there is likely to be little respite from more volatile weather until 2022, at the earliest. The author of the paper, Florian Sévellec who works for the French National Centre for Scientific Research, has built a forecasting system based on statistical 'hind-casting', which involves looking at which previous climate models worked best in the prediction of past trends in temperature. Whereas from 1998 to 2010, natural cooling worked to keep global warming in check, the world has moved into a phase where the ocean circulation and weather systems are actually set to drive temperatures up.

Sévellec's number crunching predicts that with faster warming oceans, there could be more typhoons, floods and hurricanes. He said:"There is a high possibility that we will be at the peak of a warm phase for the next couple of years" and "What we don't always feel is global warming. As a scientist, this is frightening because we don't consider it enough. All we can do is give people information and let them make up their own

None-the-less, prolonged periods of heat during the summer months (whilst not a given) are an increasing probability, especially over the next few years when cyclical natural phenomena will effectively amplify global warming extremes (see left). Whilst sunshine is preferable to rain, many weeks of it (and soaring temperatures to boot) can be incredibly problematic for gardens, as many of us experienced in 2018.

As well as the time-consuming burden of dealing with the endless back and forth of watering to try and keep plants suitably quenched, the heat stress of such prolonged, high temperatures, especially for those areas of the garden in direct sunlight, can cause immediate damage. In the short term, plants may appear stunted or stop growing all together, while others wilt and die.

In the longer term, the stress of dealing with the heat can weaken plants that had otherwise (to all outward appearances) managed to survive. In such cases, stress can hamper a plant's ability to cope with further extremes, such as those potentially thrown at us in winter.

Alongside reconsidering and revising the planting that we use in the future and growing for resilience, there are some quick and easy measures we can take to provide protection and prepare for the next time we experience such searing tropical heat.

Watering plants early or late in the day allows the water to soak deeper into the soil

The how to protect your plants checklist for next time a heatwave strikes

Watering at the right time of day A soaking either early in the morning or later at night will enable water to permeate much deeper into the soil to the benefit of your plants. Once the thermostat starts to rise, plants will start transpiring and some of your precious resource, and the time spent delivering it, will simply evaporate away.

Water for longer, less often Rather than a surface watering, go for a longer soaking, so that the water seeps deep into the soil and stays around for longer. When you consider that the soil's surface forms the front line, enduring the heat of the sun, it makes sense to ensure your plants have access to water deep in the ground around their roots. This way less day-to-day watering will be necessary.

Mulch thirstier plants Not all plants have the same requirements, so those with a greater

KIM ON GARDENING WITH A VERY LIMITED WATER SUPPLY

Like many smallholders, my water comes from a private bore hole and not the mains supply. Whilst this flummoxed me more than a little when I first moved from the city nine years ago, I was assured (and shown evidence) that the supply of water on the land was solid and viable to support the house and gardens all year round.

That it did for many years, until the heatwave of 2018 when it promptly dried out almost entirely. I could see it happening slowly but surely as the water tank took longer and longer to fill. Finally, we got down to a slow trickle, which was barely enough to flush the toilets in the house let alone anything else, and certainly not with any surplus for the gardens and polytunnels I have on my land.

Thankfully, with community bartering spirit in good supply in my neck of the Welsh woods, my farming neighbours agreed to bring water round in a tank every few days in exchange for a supply of fruit and vegetables from the garden. Not wanting to milk this goodwill to the detriment of neighbourly relations,

combined with the fact that accessing this water supply involved a lot of too-ing and fro-ing with buckets, I decided that my gardens simply had to make do with very little in the way of refreshments. Instead, I saw it as a way of testing my climate change gardening skills to the limit. The polytunnels had to survive with a watering just once a week, whilst the veg patch, shrubs and other plants were only watered a handful of times over the summer months.

Whilst some produce struggled with the severe shortage of watering, especially cucumbers and fennel, most thrived surprisingly well because of the measures I had in place to make the best use of the water. I've never watered so little before! While gardeners up and down the country were bemoaning the amount of work involved in keeping their gardens quenched, I was able to use the experience to assess firsthand how resilient a lot of plants and crops can actually be with just a little care and attention along the way.

Right: Kim's garden coped well with little water

Calendula creates ground cover in a polytunnel

THE **CLIMATE CHANGE** GARDEN

Scrambling nasturtium covers the ground

Gravel acts as a mulch too

thirst can be protected by way of a surface mulch around their base. Compost enables soil to hold onto a greater volume of water than it would be able to otherwise, so it's a first choice in this regard for a mulch, although other materials can also be used (see page 66).

If you water before applying the mulch, the moisture will stay in the ground for even longer, protected by the layer above.

Building longer term resilience against heatwaves

We have some easy suggestions for you to help build drought resilience in your garden.

Choose your planting wisely Some plants simply have greater resilience and are especially drought-hardy. Trees, shrubs and long-lived perennials tend to have deeper roots, which enable them to seek out moisture from a much wider area. You can read more about this topic in the later chapters.

Use ground cover During the summer months, it's important to providing ground cover around more vulnerable plants. This really really does come into its own during a heatwave. Protecting the soil from the sun with leaves and mulch helps to maintain the moisture levels to the benefit of surrounding plants (You can read more on mulching in chapter 4).

Also worth considering are other forms of

Taller crops on the veg plot will shade others

A trellis of hops shades a path

ground cover, including bark, wood chip and even gravel gardens have their place when it comes to keeping moisture where you need it most. (See chapter 4 and also the gravel garden on page 188)

Use planting as shelter A south-facing garden will be in the front line when it comes to the impact of intense sunshine. We don't want to block out the light altogether, but creating some areas of partial shade can be useful. This can be done by carefully positioning taller plants, such as sunflowers, Jerusalem artichokes, or a trellis of climbing

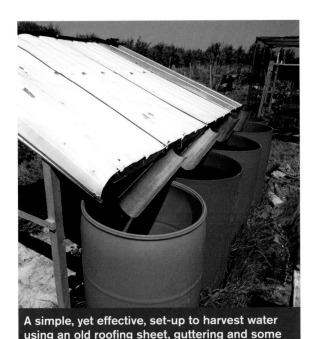

A simple, yet effective, set-up to harvest water using an old roofing sheet, guttering and some ubiquitous blue barrels.

Harvesting water from a greenhouse roof means there is a handy store of water nearby

plants so that they cast shade over smaller plants. New trees can also be used to cast natural shade over the house (see chapter 9).

Build resilience in your soil By ensuring your soil is of the best possible quality, its ability to hold and retain water will be greatly enhanced. Not digging the soil will further enable the beneficial community of bacteria and fungi to work their natural magic, providing a greater resilience to extremes of weather.

Water harvesting

In the midst of winter when rain is in ample supply, it's hard to imagine how precious this resource might become in the months ahead.

A typical suburban roof could collect as much as 24,000 litres (5,280 gallons) of water in a year, that's enough to fill 150 water butts, assuming you had the storage space! This brings home the sheer volume of this natural resource that is available for harvesting during the wetter months of the year.

VALUABLE DIPPING PONDS

Some years ago when constructing her raised bed vegetable garden Sally decided to build a formal dipping pond. She had seen them in traditional gardens and thought them a useful addition. The pond was lined with fibreglass to give an extra long life and took a downpipe from a nearby barn and had an overflow going into a natural pond outside of the vegetable garden.

It proved its worth in 2018. Starting the year full, the water lasted the whole season, getting down to the last 10cm just before the drought broke. Another feature of a dipping pond, as the name suggests, is the ease of dipping a bucket or watering can in the water and to have it full instantly – no more waiting to fill it up, saving valuable minutes when watering the beds. During 2018 a myriad of visitors were seen at the pond, including birds and dragonflies.

Certainly, the contents of any standard-sized water butt run out quickly during a prolonged period of drought, and not many back gardens have room above ground for more than one or two of these collection vessels.

Making the most of grey water from general household use is another viable option. From paddling pool to bath water, the amount of this precious resource that is used up and flushed away is undoubtedly rather staggering, were we to measure it. Yet a simple pump can be used effectively to channel water from water butts and elsewhere into your garden, where it can be put to a valuable second use.

Planning for the future

If you are moving into a new-build house and have some cash to spend on the garden, a wise investment would be an extensive water harvesting system with an underground water storage tank. If you are lucky, you may even find that the builders have already integrated a rainwater-harvesting system into the property.

The problem with a standard butt is that it holds up to around 300 litres (66 gallons), so will fill quickly after heavy rain. The only way to harvest more water is to have a row of butts. Even a large 1,000 litre (220 gallons) tank will be quickly filled by a roof area of just 30m² (323 ft²). There is also a risk of frost damage as the water inside will freezing during a cold spell. An underground tank can store as much as 10,000 litres (2,200 gallons) of water, and sometimes more, so that's a considerable improvement. Being underground, it takes up no space in the garden and the water remains cool. It is fitted with a pump so that water can be used for irrigating the garden.

Different ways of watering

Where possible, you want to water the soil around your plants (and deeply). The quickest and most efficient way to do this is through a hand held spray gun, which allows you to direct the water away from foliage (where it will soon burn off) and to soak into the soil where it will stay around for longer.

If you have the space or a new garden, future-proof your water supply by installing underground tanks

Watering cans will also enable you to control the direction of the flow but are very time consuming in the process.

Sprinkler systems are often used in poly-tunnels and for lawns, and enable you to flick a switch, turn a tap and go. They also enable you to accurately measure the amount of time spent watering, so it can be adjusted according to the requirements of the day. They aren't the most efficient systems, however in terms of water use, as everything gets a soak in the vicinity, including pathways and foliage, but they are quick and easy to work with. In the future, as the cost of water rises you might

A hand held spray gun is a quick way of watering veg beds

want to look for more efficient options.

Slow seeping systems are popular and can work well during the summer months, especially for water-hungry crops and plants in large pots. The slow drip ensures a sufficient supply of water at this warmer time of year.

These systems are also easy to connect to a water butt and can be done so often without the need for the purchase of an additional pump. However, the slowness of the drip throughout the day will mean that some of the water will evaporate and be wasted during a heatwave.

Learning from the past

Burying pots

Water is bound to become more expensive and with the likelihood of hosepipe bans being more commonplace, we need to look at different approaches. One efficient and ancient method of irrigation, used by small-scale subsistence farmers in the drier parts of the world, is based on buried, unglazed clay pots, called ollas, which are filled with water. These have a short, but wide neck, and wide body which makes them look like a beanpot. Being porous, water passes out of the pot when the surrounding soil is dry, so the rate of irrigation is dependent on the plant's water use. It's a highly efficient method compared with drip irrigation and surface irrigation and is well suited to use in the greenhouse or polytunnel. You can buy these pots online now, but you could adapt a clay pot by bunging up the drainage holes and using a clay saucer as a cover.

This system of buried pots doesn't need a pressurised water supply, is less likely to be damaged and the pots don't need filling every day, just once a week or so. It's targeted irrigation so you are not watering the ground. To install, dig a hole that's wider and deeper than the ollas, fork soil around hole to aid drainage, mix in 1/3 compost or manure, plus some sand or grit to improve drainage. Place the pot in the hole so its rim lies just above surface, gently firm soil in place fill water and

Pop a lid on the pot to stop animals getting in

cover. The pot spacing depends on the crops, 1–1.5m (3'3"–4'11") apart for sweetcorn and other tall plants, 1m (3'3") apart for tomatoes. Water regularly and don't let it dry out as this will slow down the delivery of water when you refill. This system works best with well-established transplants as their roots have better chance of reaching water. It's also wise to set up the system early in the season before the natural water reservoir in the soil has been depleted and plants can get established. Add a mulch to reduce evaporation further. It works well for most crops, especially spreading plants that create ground cover, but very thirsty plants, such as spinach and squash, may not get enough on hot days. Also, check that it's not delivering too much water during wet spells creating moisture that favours mould.

CHAPTER
THREE

WIND, FROST AND SNOW

Even if you don't live up high in an exposed location prone to strong winds and a greater battering from the elements in general, the increase in the number of storms and potential for frost and snow later (or indeed earlier) in the season means these are prospective weather events to be very mindful of indeed.

Not wild about wind

It's referred to in some circles as the gardener's foe, as it can cause so much damage to planting in a short space of time. At lower speeds, wind performs a valuable service, blowing the cobwebs (and indeed fungal diseases) well and truly away. It's for good reason, as enabling sufficient air flow provides good ventilation within a polytunnel or greenhouse, which is essential to the health and vitality of indoor-grown plants. Outside, of course, this happens naturally: it's just that it sometimes occurs too often and too vigorously.

Even on a warm spring day, the temperature around your planting can, in reality, be significantly colder due to the cooling effect of the wind. As well as potentially stunting the growth of seedlings early in year, through the dip in temperature, wind can also have

Strong winds cause loss of roadside trees

a drying effect on foliage (known as wind scorch). It results in the browning of leaves, especially those of evergreens, which are most susceptible to damage. It can cause branches and foliage to rip and tear, and in extreme situations, can result in trees being uprooted and overturned, which can cause damage to surrounding planting and occasionally people's homes.

There are many things that can be done, however, to provide a degree of protection for your garden or allotment against excessively strong wind, even in the most exposed of locations.

Plant wind breaks

Ideally, you want to plant trees or bushes as a wind break, rather than a complete barrier

CASE STUDY

KIM'S WINDPROOFED GARDEN

My garden lies in a very exposed location, more than 200m (700') above sea level and westerly winds, in particular, can be problematic. To provide protection, an outer layer of mixed trees have been planted at the back of the site, with a range of fruit trees and soft fruits located to provide a further natural barrier in front. This is topped off with fast-growing willow at the top of the veg patch. This multi-layered defence ensures that the produce and plants in the central gardens are much better able to ride out storms.

as this will take the sting out of the gale by slowing it down. A solid barrier would reflect the wind away to potentially causing damage elsewhere, which is why solid walls and fencing are less desirable. Such planting provides a natural protection against the wind and has additional benefits in that it can help to soak up excess rainfall. Green windbreaks also have deep, wide-ranging roots, which help bind the surrounding soil together. Suitable species in this regard include:

- Birch (*Betula*)
- Escallonia (*Escallonia*)
- False acacia (*Robinia*)
- Hawthorn (*Crateagus*)
- Holly (*Ilex*)
- Laurel (*Laurus nobilis*)
- Leylandii (*Cupressus x leylandii*)
- Magnolia (*Magnolia grandiflora*)
- Oleaster or silverberry (*Elaeagnus x submacrophylla*)

Jerusalem artichoke provides a useful summer windbreak

A row of crab apples creates an attractive wind break

- Sea buckthorn (*Hippophae rhamnoides*)
- Sycamore (*Acer pseudoplatinus*)
- Willow (*Salix*)

Annual windbreaks

On the veg patch, taller produce such as cardoon, sunflowers, Jerusalem artichokes and even runner beans can be used to provide a degree of protection.

Attractive windbreak planting

The likes of willow, bamboo and grasses can form an elegant, ornamental wind break in the garden and they can look extremely attractive as they are blown hither and thither by the wind. Another option to consider are fruit bushes and trees to provide both functional and edible protection.

Other methods of wind protection

There are some other options that can be useful in the battle against the wind. Trellis, with its spaced lattices, works to slow, rather than deflect the wind, while an archway or pergola populated with climbing plants can provide another aesthetically-pleasing defence.

More drastic measures include the creation of a windbreak bank, which is essentially a mound of earth to deflect wind up and over your garden. It can be planted with hardy perennials to make an attractive and functional garden feature.

Storm SOS check list

So you've heard that a severe storm is on the way, and you are worried that it will cause damage to your garden. To help further shore up your defences, here's what to do:

- Move any pots with tall plants inside, or to a more sheltered spot of your garden
- Protect taller produce on the veg patch (such as sweetcorn and sunflowers) by adding some bamboo canes for staked and tied support
- If you have any top-heavy plants, these could be trimmed back to reduce their wind resistance and help them ride out the storm
- Move any lightweight garden furniture into a garage or other secure place

- If you have a polytunnel, make sure the doors are closed securely and cannot blow around. Also, check there are no objects lying around the tunnel that could be picked up by the wind and damage the plastic, and that everything is neat and tidy inside, as the wind can pick up objects inside as well as out.

It's snow joke

Picture postcard images of the ideal British winter frequently feature a snow-covered landscape, with maybe some brightly coloured berries and a robin valiantly braving the cold. In reality, snow itself can actually work to provide a protective insulation, even to the ground and plants buried below it. You just have to think of an igloo to understand how snow can offer protection to plants. And of course, in winter, plants are generally prepared for the cold, having died back or gone into dormancy.

However, changes in weather patterns and the increased volatility that go with them now mean that snow can arrive much later in the year; well into spring, in fact. This late uninvited arrival can cause a lot of damage. At this time of year, plants are beginning to grow new shoots and blossom, and many of these delicate structures simply can't tolerate extremes of cold. New growth will be killed, weakening the plant in the process, and even killing the more cold-sensitive species.

A suburban garden during a snow storm

THE **CLIMATE CHANGE** GARDEN

Snow on a polytunnel or greenhouse should be removed to prevent tearing or cracking of the overburdened cover materials.

Here's what you can do to help:

- Prune less on tender plants
- Older foliage and growth can provide a degree of protection for the crown of a plant and help it weather a cold snap (as well as proving a potential overwintering habitat for wildlife)
- Choose your planting areas wisely. The lowest area of your garden will be the most susceptible to becoming a frost pocket, so bear this in mind when deciding where to plant in the first place. It's best to avoid this location altogether for frost sensitive plants.
- Protect your pots, whether it's moving them

indoors, or just choosing frost-proof materials to prevent cracking or splitting when the cold weather strikes, it's best to be prepared in advance.

- In the case of heavy snow, the weight of these ice crystals can cause damage to the branches and leaves of trees and shrubs. In the case of a heavy dusting, it's best to brush them off to avoid damage.

Risk from frost

As the climate warms up, it's likely that we will experience fewer frosty mornings, but there is always the risk of unusual weather patterns bringing a particularly early or late frost. Frosts form on clear, cold nights when the air temperatures fall and excess water vapour in the air condenses out to form dew on the surface of plant leaves. If the temperatures drop below freezing, the dew freezes to form a frost, with the cooling continuing when the sun rises again in the morning.

What's a frost pocket?

We may hear gardeners tutt-tutting about frost pockets and frost hollows but what do they mean?

It's basically land that has a higher risk of suffering from frost overall and is therefore more likely to be at risk from this either early or late in the year; both of which are bad news if you are growing some of the less hardy plants in your garden. When temperatures fall

Cabbages are frost hardy

This dahlia was damaged by an early frost

at night, the cold air sinks to the ground and flows downhill and collect in hollows in the landscape that enables it to hang around for longer. Sometimes the cold air may be trapped by a hedge, fence or wall. If you know you have a frost hollow you can help by making gaps in the barrier at the lowest point so the cold air can flow away, or you can prevent the cold air flowing into your garden by putting up a line of shrubs or trees.

Frost damage

The damage caused by frost varies according to the hardiness of the plant concerned. For example, a subtropical plant won't tolerate any frost, but a hardy winter-resilient species can probably cope with weeks of freezing weather. A hardy plant can survive, either because it is dormant in the ground, or the freezing point of its cells' content is much lower, so the cells do not freeze. You can read more about plant hardiness-chart in the Appendix (see page 212).

Ultimately, each garden has its own microclimate, so temperatures will vary from one side to the other and, if you garden on a slope, the bottom of the incline is likely to be more prone to frost than the top. This is, therefore, an important determining factor when it comes to deciding where in the garden you position some of your less hardy plants.

The physical damage from frost is caused when the water within cells freezes. When water freezes, the liquid turns to ice crystals and it expands by approximately 9%. It's this expansion that ruptures the plant cell walls, damaging the plant in the process. Plants are particularly vulnerable to late spring frosts, because, if they get early morning sun, this can warm up the plant too rapidly which can also damage the leaves. Should you find a plant has been frosted, you can spray it with cold water before the sun reaches it and this will help reduce the degree of harm caused. Try not to cut back perennials before winter as the old shoots will actually work to provide protection for the plant until spring. For the same reason, it's best to wait until the risk of frost has passed before pruning shrubs.

If you know a late frost is forecast you can:

- Cover small fruit trees and trained trees on walls with a fleece at night to protect the blossom
- Wrap vulnerable container plants with fleece
- Cover small plants with a cloche
- A well watered soil holds more heat than dry soil, so water a seed bed or young transplants early in the day and then cover them with a fleece
- Avoid hoeing on a day that frost is forecast as hoeing has been found to lower the surface temperature of the soil overnight by several degrees.

Kales such as cavolo nero are tolerant of frost

How to save damaged plants

Is there anything that can be done to save a frost-blackened plant in the garden?

Well, if it's a soft-stemmed plant, remove the frost-damaged shoots as they may rot and cause more problems. For a woody plant, you can leave the frosted shoots until spring, when the last risk of frost has passed. Then prune all the dead stems. The living stem should start to grow back in time. As with plants that have suffered from flood damage, you can encourage new growth with a fertiliser boost.

CHAPTER
FOUR

A HEALTHY SOIL

The soil in our gardens may not be glamorous or indeed exciting to look at. It's easy to take for granted the stuff in which we dig holes to prop up our plants. Yet, in reality it's so incredibly important when it comes to building resilience against climate change. A healthy, nutrient-rich loam is at the heart of matters no less. It should be at the front line in our efforts to provide protection against the increasing extremes of weather that face us.

As well as helping to mop up carbon dioxide and to forge stronger, healthier plants, soil is a living entity in its own right. There is a complex web of inter-dependent microorganisms living within it and they need to be looked after. There is a vital connection between soil, plants, animals, people and the planet. For example, a compost-rich soil has an improved structure that enables it to absorb and retain more water than it would be able to otherwise. That's very handy when you consider that our precious soil has to stand firm against the future weather, which could include deluges of rain, alongside periods of searing heat and drought.

With higher summer temperatures in the future, the soil will be warmer and there will be more evaporation of water from the soil's surface and plant leaves. Plant roots will need to take up more water to replenish the losses. in fact, a rise of 3°C (5.4°F) by 2080 could see the average soil moisture content reduced by as much as a quarter. So, a healthy soil is at the top of the list of things we should be aiming for in our gardens.

How can you achieve a healthy soil? We are going to guide you through the components that make up soil and the life within it, and outline simple, yet effective ways to nurture and improve your soil to the benefit of your climate change garden.

What's in soil?

Soil is a mix of minerals, organic matter, air, water and living organisms. The minerals – sand, silt and clay – make up almost half of soil and they come from the breakdown of rocks. The organic matter comes from the breakdown of dead and decaying matter, while the spaces between all the particles are filled by air or water. The ability of soil to retain water depends largely on its texture. Soils containing more of the smaller clay and silt particles can hold much more water than a sandy soil with much larger particles.

Why is organic matter important?

Soils vary in their organic matter content. Organic matter is important as it forms a reservoir of nutrients, so the amount of organic matter present in soil is an indicator of fertility. The organic matter helps soil particles to clump together and form aggregates and this improves the structure of the soil, which in turn, improves permeability and the ability of soil to hold water. Organic matter acts like a sponge, holding up to 10 times its weight in water, which can be used by plants.

The vital component

Living organisms make up less than 1% of the soil volume, but they are a vital part of soil. They range in size from bacteria to earthworms. Bacteria and fungi are key to the decomposition of organic materials, while specialist bacteria take on other roles. The nitrogen fixers, for example, take nitrogen from the air and convert it to nitrates that plants can use. Some nitrogen fixers are free-living in the soil, while others are found in the root nodules of leguminous plants, such as peas and beans.

Also important are the mycorrhizal fungi that are associated with plant roots. A mycorrhizal fungus supplies a plant with nutrients, while the plant supplies the fungus with sugar. Mycorrhizal fungi have a very large network of thread-like hyphae that extend out from the plant roots enabling the fungus to source nutrients and water from a much larger volume of soil than the plant could do itself.

Climate change will affect soil life too. As temperatures increase, biological activity will increase. Soil microbes will be active for longer as spring arrives ever earlier and winters are milder, and this may lead to more a rapid breakdown of dead and decaying materials, so more nutrients may be available to plants.

Quick healthy soil check – do you have earthworms?

The presence of earthworms is a great indicator of soil life and health. Earthworm numbers decline if the soil is compacted, waterlogged, too acidic, or has been rotavated or turned, but their numbers increase if there is plenty of organic matter in the soil. The best time of year to count earthworms is in early autumn or late spring, times when earthworms are active and can be found in the upper layers of soil. It helps to carry out the count after warm, wet conditions too.

Dig a soil pit about 20 x 20 x10cm (8"x 8"x4") and place the soil on a tray or plastic bag. Break up the soil and collect all the earthworms. Count the total number plus the number of adults and juveniles. Size doesn't tell you about maturity, as earthworm species vary in length. An adult earthworm is identified by the presence of a saddle, which is a thickened ring of segments about a third of its length from the head (pointed end). A healthy soil will have 10 to 15 earthworms in the block. Once counted, put all the earthworms back in the hole with the soil.

It can be useful to look in more detail at the types of earthworms in your garden. There are 31 species of earthworm in Britain according to the Earthworm Society of Britain (although many are rare), and they are grouped into three types: anecic, endogeic and epigeic, each with a specific role. You can download earthworm identification sheets from the internet and see what earthworms are in your garden.

- Anecic earthworms are deep burrowers, more than 8cm (3") long and dark red in colour. They make deep vertical burrows and create earthworm casts. They are the typical 'earthworm' that are active at night looking for leaf litter, which they pull into their burrow. Their burrows help soil drainage and aeration so their presence is important.

- Endogeic are small to medium length earthworms, pale coloured or green in appearance and with a tendency to curl up when handled. These earthworms have a role in soil aggregation.

- Epigeic earthworms are found mostly in the leaf litter. They are small, roughly the size of matchsticks, dark red in colour and fast moving.

Take a good look at your soil

A typical wedge of soil

Take a good look at your soil

Before you can improve your soil, you need to know what soil type it is and if there are any issues, such as compaction, so it's wise to carry out a few basic tests. Here are three tests that you can carry out really easily.

1. Soil texture

Take a handful of soil and squeeze it. What does it feel like? Sandy soil will feel gritty and won't hold its shape but fall away, whereas a handful of clay-rich soil will feel wetter, slippery and hold its shape. If it's something in-between, then you have a loam – a mix of all three particle sizes. The ribbon test is easy too. Roll some soil between your fingers and thumb. If you can squeeze it into a ribbon that's 6 cm (2.5") long or more, it's rich in clay. A shorter ribbon indicates a loam, while soil that won't form a ribbon at all is rich in sand.

2. Slake test

Slaking is the breakdown of large soil aggregates into smaller aggregates when suddenly immersed in water. It tests the soil's crumb structure, the slower the soil breaks up, the more organic matter present. Take a handful of soil and place in a bag. Fill a shallow dish with rainwater and place on the side. Select

Biochar

Sally is fascinated by biochar and the potential it offers to the climate change garden. Biochar has long been made in the Amazon by indigenous tribes and used to improve the productivity of their soil. Plant matter is placed trenches, covered with soil and burnt slowly in low oxygen conditions to make a charcoal. Today, biochar is sold as a soil amendment. It's made in the same way, from plant biomass by pyrolysis; that's burning at high temperatures without oxygen to create a black material that is rich in carbon. It looks solid, but it's filled with lots of microscopic holes, so it's porous and rigid and has a huge surface area.

Mixing biochar into soil has many useful benefits: it improves aeration, reduces the risk of compaction and holds on to soluble mineral nutrients so there is no leaching. Soil microbes shelter in the particles and hide from larger predators, so the number of beneficial fungi and bacteria within can be 10 times more than in soil without biochar. One property that is important for a climate change garden is biochar's ability to hold onto water. It seeps through the honeycomb of holes and does not drain away, boosting the moisture-holding capacity of the ground. Research shows that the use of a biochar-amended soil around transplanted saplings leads to greater survival rates as it improves the plants' ability to withstand drought.

Biochar can also help efforts to counter climate change as it locks up carbon so there is less carbon dioxide compared with burning plant biomass or leaving it to rot. In fact, the formation of one tonne of biochar from wood removes three tonnes of carbon from the atmosphere.

How much biochar to add? It's almost a case of the more the better. Some people say a thin layer on top of soil is a good start. Another way is to mix biochar into your compost as you add it as a surface dressing. Dug in or left on top, either way it will boost soil health. You can mix it into the compost used for potted plants at the rate of 100g per 4 litres (4 ounces per gallon) of compost or into raised beds. Permaculturalists say it's important to 'biocharge' the biochar to get accelerated growth of mycorrhizal fungi by mixing biochar into your compost heap so that its full of microorganisms before it goes on the soil.

three pea-sized lumps of soil and using a teaspoon gently place the lumps in the water, spaced equidistant. After two hours record by how much the lumps have broken up and then again after 24 hours. Those soils with aggregates that hold together have more organic matter, which helps to bind the soil particles

and they are more able to maintain their structure during wet weather. These soils are more resistant to erosion and can maintain their structure, providing air and water for plants.

3. Percolation test
The percolation test looks at drainage. Dig

Learning from the past

Dry farming

Dry farming is farming with little or no supplemental water and is practiced in the western USA, Mexico, Mediterranean countries, on volcanic islands such as Lanzarote, parts of Australia and even by the Incas more than 11,000 years ago. We can learn so much from these methods and apply them to our own gardens.

The formal definition of dry farming is growing crops during a dry season using the residual moisture in the soil accumulated during the wetter parts of year and with no additional irrigation. It's not a method to maximise production, but a sustainable one since yields are much lower. Grapes are the traditional dry farmed crop as their roots extend deep into the ground in search of water and minerals. Dry farmers have various strategies to conserve soil moisture: incorporation of organic matter, no tillage/

no dig and mulching, combined with the use of drought-resistant varieties and carefully timed planting. Key to success is soil type and water-holding-capacity as it's not possible to use these methods on well-drained sandy soils with little organic matter. Native Americans of the desert states of the United States, such as the Hopi, were farmers for thousands of years and coped with the intermittent winter rains and grew drought-resistant crops, such as maize (Hopi blue corn). They harvested water during storms by building a series of canals to direct the water to shallow beds where the crops where grown.

On the volcanic Canary Islands, farmers build small walls of lava rocks around their beds to create shelter and trap condensation from fog. Similarly, West African growers build low earth berms around key plants to trap water and provide shade from sun and wind, which helps seedlings to get established.

a square hole about 30cm (12") across and 30cm (12") deep. Fill the hole with water and allow it to drain away. Record how long it takes for the water to drain away. Ideally, you are looking for a soil that allows water to drain away in two to four hours, anything outside of this range this means you need to take some remedial action. If drainage times are very slow, even as much as 10 hours, you may have compaction and a hard pan under the top soil is stopping the water from draining away.

A slow-draining soil is liable to waterlog and this can lead to the death of plant roots. In contrast, if the water drains away in an hour or less, the soil is very sandy. Any water will drain away from the plant roots too quickly and in dry weather the plants will need a lot of watering.

A well-drained soil

We'll be using the term 'a well-drained soil' a lot. It describes a soil that has a good structure with lots of air spaces that allow water to per-colate through at a reasonable speed, neither too quickly nor too slowly.

Drainage is one of the most important factors in making your garden climate-change resil-ient. It is difficult to tell just from looking at soil how well drained it is, but if your soil is always soggy and puddles lie around for several hours after rain, you've got poor draining soil (see percolation test above).

The soil type in your garden determines which types of plants you will be able to grow and gives you an indication of the problems that you might encounter during extreme weather.

Sandy soils are great when it rains heavily as the water drains quickly, but in a hot and dry summer, these soils are going to dry out more quickly and require watering or mulching. Clay soils hold water in winter and are prone to waterlogging, while in summer they dry up and become hard and difficult to work, but they do hold on to water for longer.

Improving drainage

Organic matter is usually the answer to better drainage. Adding organic matter, such as compost, to a sandy soil will improve its structure and allow more water to be retained. Similarly, mixing organic matter into a heavy clay soil will also improve its structure, helping water move through the soil more quickly and reducing drainage times. If you have particularly heavy clay the soil may benefit from grit too.

Mulching

Something else that's recommended for improving your garden's resilience is mulching – the spreading of a layer of loose material over the surface of soil.

The benefits of mulching are many:
- it helps to retain moisture in summer

Readily available mulches include:

Grass clippings A low fertility option, spread thinly over the soil after watering or rain, do bear in mind that too thick a layer will create a foul-smelling mat of rotting grass. Yet a small application retains moisture and suppresses weeds. Some people allow the clippings to dry first before adding a thicker layer over the soil. It's important to always check first that the lawn from which the clipping have been taken, hasn't been treated with chemicals such as weed killer!

Wood chip, sawdust, bark, pine needles Some people argue that these materials rob the soil of nitrogen, but research has found that if they are mulched rather than dug in, they are fine to use. They quickly form a layer that suppresses weeds and reduces evaporation. In time, they will rot down and boost the organic matter.

Be careful with sawdust as it has a tendency to create a mat, but it can be used to create a water-permeable path. If you are using conifer-wood chips, take care not to mulch around young plants and just use it around established plants as the tannins in the conifer material are phytotoxic and can inhibit the growth of young plants. Also, if you are using chipped materials supplied by a tree surgeon, it's important to ensure you do not use woody materials from plants suffering from bacterial canker or honey fungus.

Shreddings A good source of mulch, spread thinly over the soil surface.

Leaf mould Place leaves in a one-tonne-bulk bag or in a wire-netting compost bin and leave them until they have rotted down to create leaf mould, but be aware that this can be a slow process, taking as long as two years. Leaf mould is not as rich in nutrients as compost, which is why it's used to make potting compost. It's also a great stimulant for soil microorganisms.

Ramial woodchips These are made from young branches no larger than 7 cm (2.7") in diameter. This wood has more nutrients and less lignin that older wood, so it's easier and quicker for fungal decomposers to break it down. Michael Phillips, author of *The Holistic Orchard* has found that ramial wood chip mulch can lead to healthier trees.

Wool fleece A layer of fleece spread over the soil will reduce water loss and suppress weeds. It is claimed that it is a good barrier for slugs and snails as they don't like moving over it. A layer of wool can be used to reduce water loss from pots in summer and provide insulation in winter.

Inert materials There is a range of inert materials that can be spread over soil and used in pots, including gravel, pebbles, glass chippings, slate, shingle, crushed shells, plastic sheeting and landscape fabric etc.

- suppresses weeds
- shelters plant roots from excessive high temperatures
- helps water penetrate the soil rather than running off the surface

All sorts of materials can be used as a mulch, some inert and others that rot down. Organic materials that rot have the additional benefits that they will improve to the soil organic matter, supply nutrients, boost drainage and water-holding-capacity and encourage micro-organisms. Biodegradable mulches include compost, wood chippings, sawdust, leaf shreddings, leaf mould, bark, manure, straw, hemp, wool fleece, seaweed, grass clippings and shredded paper.

When to mulch

You can apply mulch all year round as you want to avoid leaving soil bare as much as possible, as it's more vulnerable to the elements when left exposed. However, the optimum time is autumn when you can spread the mulch after harvesting your crops. Mulch keeps the soil covered during winter and stops weed seeds from germinating, plus micro-organisms have plenty of time to get to work before you sow the next crop.

Mulching around shrubs and trees will also suppress weeds and create a moisture-retentive layer, but don't spread the mulch right up to the trunks as it can set up points susceptible to rot. You can add a mulch anytime from

Vertical mulching

This sounds odd, but you can improve the infiltration of water through the soil by pushing the stiff stems of sweetcorn or sunflower deep into the ground to create a pathway for water to move freely. In the same way, you can use a tool to create a narrow vertical hole which you can backfill with sand. We come back to this method again on page 174.

late spring through summer when needed. If the weather is dry, water the soil first and then spread your mulch.

Composting

One of the most useful things you could do to create a more resilient garden is to make your own compost. This crumbly, dark, earthy-smelling material is the perfect soil amendment for mulching and adding nutrients to your soil and its nature's way of recycling all your garden waste. If you have a tiny garden and no space for a compost bin, then you can buy compost from local green waste schemes, but its far better to make your own.

Gardeners tend to have their own tried and tested way of making compost. Some simply pile it up and let nature take over. Others have a far more scientific approach, mixing up different materials and regularly turning the

Learning from the past

Mulching, no work and no dig

The 'no-work, deep mulch' method of gardening goes back to Ruth Stout in the US. Ruth Stout was born in Kansas in 1884 and much of her gardening was devoted to labour-saving methods and her book titles reflect that, *How to have a green thumb without an aching back* and *Gardening without work*. Her 'no-work, deep mulch' method was to keep a thick mulch (20 cm / 8") of biodegradable matter on the vegetable and flower beds all year round. As she explained: 'as it decays, it enriches the soil' and she would continually add more. She claims never to have used a plough, spade or hoe, or to have cultivated, weeded, watered, sprayed, sowed a cover crop or built a compost heap – so she really did break the rules.

All sorts of organic materials were used to mulch her beds, including hay, straw, leaves, pine needles, sawdust, vegetable peelings, in fact anything that would rot. She sowed directly into the mulch, moving the mulch back to drop in the seeds and then covering them over again. During the year, if she saw weeds popping through she added a handful of hay – so she mulched whenever needed.

Sally saw this method used on one of the allotments on her organic farm. An allotmenteer covered his plot with a really thick layer of old hay and straw in spring and then made infrequent visits to sow seeds, transplant seedlings and to harvest. There was no watering and the occasional weeding – a truly low maintenance method that yielded great results. From reports of people using the method in the US, it works well in the hottest of summers, requires little or no watering and it's good for growing vegetables on poor soils, such as sand and heavy clay.

Ruth Stout's deep mulch approach was the forerunner of the no-till or no dig methods used around the world and made popular in recent years by Eliot Coleman and Lee Reich in the US and Charles Dowding in the UK. The no-till or no-dig method is one in which the soil is left undisturbed and each year the soil is top-dressed with a layer of compost, in the same way as a layer of leaf litter covers woodland soils each year. The advantages of this method are many: the compost layer covers and protects the soil, smothers weeds and boosts organic content and water retention. In time, the soil builds up more organic matter, has a better water relationship

Good use has been made of mulch

Planting into thick mulch

between plants and soil, the earthworms and network of fungal hyphae are undisturbed as is the capillary structure of the soil. In terms of water and flooding, most of the allotmenteers at Sally's farm are no-dig, and it's interesting that those who like to dig, or worse still, rotovate have seen more problems with puddling and even flooding compared with their neighbours, who apply lots of mulch.

Another technique that works well is leaving crop roots in the ground – chop off the old plants at ground level and leave the roots in the soil to hold the soil particles in place. And the other benefit of these techniques – you are locking up more carbon than you are releasing so helping in the battle to reduce carbon emissions – it may be a tiny contribution, but if every gardener did this, the effect would be great.

A biodegradable plastic film acts as a mulch

Ornamental mulch of recycled glass chippings

heap. A well-made, aerated and moist compost heap made in summer and turned regularly can convert all the organic matter to compost within a couple of months, but a typical garden compost heap that is gradually built up from layers of materials over the year will take much longer. But all are agreed that to get a compost heap off a good start you need a mix of carbon and nitrogen-rich materials. There's lots of carbon in brown materials, such as leaves, woody material, straw, newspaper, cardboard, while materials rich in nitrogen are the green things, grass clippings, coffee grounds, fresh leaves, waste from the kitchen. You need roughly half brown to half green to get the right balance – too much green and you will be left with a smelly mush, too much brown and composting will be very slow.

A basic compost bin can be as simple as four sides made from recycled pallets and a lid to keep out the rain, but you can also buy plastic bins cheaply. It's best to gather all your materials together and fill the bin in one go. Cover and leave for about a month. Then take it all out, give it a good mix and return it to the bin. Three or four months later it should be brown and crumbly. Any larger pieces of plant material can be removed and the rest used on the garden. If you are filling the bin as you garden, then the heap won't get as hot so will take longer, but it will get there in the end.

TIP

Allowing the bottom of your compost pile to touch the soil will enable the beneficial creatures involved in the decomposition process to make their way in. Equally, rather than meticulously turning your pile, another option to help speed the process along is the application of a layer of microbial-rich material from your compost-ready pile.

Compost – the best soil cure all?

Kim certainly believes so. Rather than testing her soil she works to the principle that the best way to improve it is through the application of a layer of compost on top. If you have a healthy loam this just needs to be done once a year.

Getting up close and personal with your precious soil by sticking your hand in and looking for earthworm activity, you can see first hand how it is faring. If your soil needs more of a helping hand, a layer of cardboard, followed by an application of a 5cm (6") layer of compost will enable you to get planting right away. It really can be as simple as that!

Why organic improves resilience

Both Sally and Kim are organic gardeners and they feel strongly that using organic methods will put us in a better position to help our gardens cope with climate change. Why? It all comes back to soil health.

Soil is an amazing ecosystem and the living component – the microorganisms, worms and other animals – is essential to plant health. Albert Howard, one of the pioneers of the organic movement, understood the link between healthy soil, healthy people, and a healthy planet. His years of research into soil and composting led him to conclude that the lower the state of fertility of the soil, the greater the likelihood of pests and diseases.

When you add an artificial fertiliser to the soil you upset the balance in the soil. It's not that the fertiliser is actually killing the soil life, unless of course, you have added so much that the levels are toxic. It's about balance. Many different types of microbes help to break down organic matter in a complex food chain and release nutrients in a form that plant roots can take up. If you add readily available nutrients, such as nitrates, this bypasses the ecosystem and the fertiliser can be taken up by the plant roots straightaway. It's disrupting the natural system. A good analogy is that an artificial fertiliser is fast food for a plant, it's a ready-to-go food. By applying the fertiliser you put all the 'artisan' microbes out of work and they start to disappear. The longer you continue to apply the fertiliser, the lower the diversity of artisan microbes in the soil. This means that you have to continue to supply fertiliser as the supply of naturally sourced nutrients is drying up and the plant won't perform quite so well without an artificial boost, so it's a catch 22. Leading soil life expert, Prof. Elaine Ingham describes soil that lacks a diversity of soil life as dirt – and that's what intensive farmers with their reliance on fertilisers are effectively working with.

The other problem with an artificial fertiliser is that it is soluble. It's ready for the plants to use, but it is easily washed away. It just takes a heavy rainstorm and nitrate fertiliser in the soil will be washed deeper beyond the plant root zone or even out onto paths and into water courses. And as we know heavy rain is going to be a more common in the future.

Obviously, the application of pesticide and weedkiller is going to adversely affect the soil microorganisms, affecting some and not others, and upsetting the balance. Even glyphosate, the one chemical we were told was not persistent and could safely be used without harming life, is proving to be harmful. The ecological safety of this chemical was not really assessed, i.e. the way it reacts with living organisms and how it is degraded by them. The manufacturers claimed it would be inactivated quickly in the soil and degraded by microbes, but now we know it is far more persistent and adversely affects soil life. The initial safety studies were carried out on just glyphosate, but glyphosate-containing weedkillers contain other substances, called adjuvants, to improve its effectiveness. Now scientists are finding that these adjuvants can be more toxic than pure glyphosate or they react with glyphosate in a way that was not predicted. The science is still confused. Studies have found that glyphosate can lower earthworm activity and reduce the viability of their cocoons leading to fewer juveniles. Some studies have found that glyphosate has no effect on bacteria, but increases numbers of fungi and actinomycetes while other studies found that repeated applications have long term effects on the balance of microbes, with those sensitive to glyphosate disappearing. Research published in 2018 found that even

Cucamelons with fleece mulch

gut bacteria in bees were harmed by glyphosate making them more prone to infection.

Combining an organic approach with techniques such as no dig, incorporating organic matter and providing soil cover help to prevent nutrient and water loss. Leaving the soil undisturbed allows fungal hyphae to remain intact holding the soil particles together and creating a network of paths through the soil, while having a high diversity of plants, wild areas, and ponds will help make your garden more resilient to pests and diseases.

CHAPTER
FIVE

DESIGN IDEAS

How we cope with increasingly volatile weather will be crucial moving forwards as we are faced with everything from acute rain and cold snaps to long periods of summer drought and soaring high temperatures. Both in the UK and the rest of the world as you have already read in this book, and no doubt picked up on in the frequent climate change news in the media, it's going to be an ongoing problem. Building resilience will therefore be key.

Thankfully this doesn't necessarily involve a complete redesign of your current gardening space, as in reality there are lots of hardiness-boosting measures and features which can be incorporated into existing layouts. They include simple things, such as raised beds and permeable paths to more complex projects, such as building swales and rain gardens. As we will outline over the coming pages it's also incredibly useful to learn from our ancestors and look back to see how gardeners coped with the big freeze of 1963 or even the Little Ice Age.

A simple raised bed

We mention raised beds a lot as they will help make your garden resilient. Why? Because they improve soil drainage, which is very important for plants that couldn't cope with waterlogged ground over winter. Also, they can raise your precious planting out of the low-lying danger zone of flooding. The ground round about your beds may become saturated,

Left: A modern design with permeable gravel paths, raised beds and water features

Despite Kim's garden being flooded, the plant roots in these raised beds were safely above the water

but unless it's very deep floodwater you're dealing with, your crops and their roots will be safely high up above, out of harm's reach. The soil in the bed also remains unaffected and there is no erosion of the nutrients within.

Additionally, another benefit of raised beds is that the soil tends to warm up more quickly in spring than the ground would do otherwise. Also, as you're working with a smaller volume of soil, it's easier to adjust conditions (such as pH) easily, allowing you to grow plants with specific requirements, such as an acidic or calcium-rich soil for example.

One potential downside of raised beds, however, is that in hot weather the soil dries more quickly and the plants may suffer, so it's important to watch the moisture levels and water if necessary. That said, using ground cover in-between planting and a mulch around especially water-hungry plants will help keep moisture where it is needed most and reduce watering requirements overall.

Raised beds made from recycled sleepers

Raised beds are typically used for vegetables but also work well for most plants. The materials from which the walls are constructed can be pretty varied; anything from stone and brick to scaffolding planks and corrugated iron, or even old tyres and glass bottles. Whilst a surround isn't essential for raised beds, having one offers many benefits, including the ability to provide over the top cover for further whatever-the-weather protection. These valuable structures are also very easy to build. Simply mark out the edge, clear any vegetation, check levels, mark corners, hammer in corner posts if these are being used and secure the boards to them. You may need retaining stakes for the sleepers and planks, also particularly deep walls may need footings. Then place a layer of thick cardboard over the soil or vegetation and back fill with soil enriched with organic matter and grit to improve drainage. If the bed is in a low-lying area or over heavy clay soil add 10 cm (4") of gravel or hardcore before backfilling. Then as a final touch, it's recommended to cover the paths around raised beds with bark, gravel or stone to create a permeable surface.

(Left) A mound bed is in the process of construction. (Right) The wood chip has been covered with a thick layer of compost and planted with a mix of vegetables

Pile it high for a drought resistant bed

Mound or hugelkultur beds, as the name suggests, are heaped beds. They are built by digging out a trench and backfilling it with a layer of woody materials, such as small logs, branches and bark to provide a long-term carbon source which is covered by more layers of wood chips and then a mix of soil and compost to create a mound which can be steep-sided or shallow. The numerous air spaces around the woody material help to retain moisture and encourage plant roots to extend deep into the ground, creating a truly drought-resilient bed.

The conditions on one side of the mound compared with the other will be different; an east-west orientation means there is a sunny side and a shadier side, while the conditions at the bottom of the bed will be different from those at the top. This allows you to plant a range of different plants. Typically, a mound bed like this is used for growing vegetables, but a shallower version could be useful in the flower garden too.

Sally was impressed with her mound bed during the drought of 2018. It wasn't watered, other than a little for newly planted veg. The Queensland Blue squash did exceptionally well compared with others grown nearby, producing 30+ m (98') of shoot growth and 12 large fruits. Its deep roots were able to reach down to the moisture trapped by the layer of rotting woody matter. Another benefit of squash is their large leaves shade the ground and this reduces evaporation from the surface of the soil.

Learning from the past

Waffle gardens

We can learn a lot from the dry farming techniques of Native American Pueblo peoples, such as the Zuni from South West USA and New Mexico. For centuries Zuni have tended resilient gardens, making use of techniques that we see today; such as the three sisters method of planting corn, squash and bean together, companion planting for pest control and even no-dig! Traditionally, they used methods that avoided disturbing the ground, just moving the soil to create a hole in which to plant and leaving the rest alone, using mulch to suppress weeds and retain moisture. Each household had a waffle garden, which was built close to the home and river for water and these gardens are still used in Arizona and New Mexico today. They are the fore-runner of the modern day one-foot square garden!

A waffle plot comprises rows of square cells separated by berms of compacted clay soil, forming a deep-walled container, which is effectively a sunken plot. When the monsoon rains come, it can't run off, but soaks into the ground. When looked at from above the cells resemble the pattern created by a waffle iron. Vegetables are planted in the cells; the shape helping to direct water onto the plants while the berms throw shade onto the plants. In addition, the Zuni built a low wall around the garden to reduce the drying effect of winds.

To make a waffle garden, you need a level site so the water flows over all of it, rather than to one side and clay soil. Clear the ground and plan your squares, typically one-foot by one-foot, but they can vary in size and shape to suit the ground. Also leave space for pathways. When the soil is wet, make the cells using hoes. Start in a corner and move the soil from the middle of the cell to the edge to build up four walls. Press the soil together to create a wall 12 to 15cm (5 to 6") high and 12 to 15cm (5 to 6") wide. Add water if the soil is too dry to mould. Once you have created a series of cells, backfill with compost but make sure there is plenty of room to add water without the water overflowing. Typically, the Zuni would use a range of soil amendments to create a fertile soil – flood plain sand, forest soil, sheep manure, and they may have mulched with gravel. And remember, you don't have to build up, you could dig down, creating a series of sunken pits, rather than raised berms.

When it comes to planting, make sure taller vegetables, such as corn, don't shade plants that like full sun. Similarly, place spreading vegetables, such as courgette or squash, at the edge so they don't scramble over other crops.

Another drought resistant idea - sunken beds

Another option is to dig down and this may be a good alternative for gardens in particularly dry areas, as a sunken bed maximises water collection as well as sheltering plants from a drying wind. They are great for keeping planting cool in a hot summer and help to retain heat in a cold winter. Plus, they can be easily watered through flood irrigation. They are traditional in the drier parts of the world, such as the southwest USA (see page 81).

From a practicality perspective, this type of bed does require a lot of effort, and indeed as you'd imagine, there's plenty of digging involved. On the plus side though you don't have to buy in materials to make one.

To get started: mark out the bed as usual and get your spade at the ready, excavating a good depth of soil, around 60cm (2'), although they can also be deeper still. Put the topsoil to one side but pile up the rest of the excavated soil around the edges of the pit to create berms (raised banks). Once it's been dug out, level the base of the bed, refill with the top soil mixed with plenty of organic matter. Fill to within 15cm (6") of the surface to allow space to mulch and water. Stamp on the berms to compress the soil so they are firm and the soil is less likely to be washed away in heavy rain and flatten the tops so you can use them as paths. If you don't have enough compost, an alternative is to use the sunken bed as a compost heap for a year,

Left: Lavender needs a freely draining soil

A permeable slate chipping path

slowly filling up the hole with organic matter till it's ready to be used.

Slow water

The 'sink it, spread it and slow it' approach to landscape design is just as applicable to your gardens as it is to cities. There are numerous ways you can slow down the flow of water across your outside space; these include permeable paths, green roofs and walls, swales, and rain gardens.

Permeable paths

A permeable path may sound quite fancy but it's not. It's simply a path that has been constructed using materials that allow water to

pass through into the ground below. Gravel, for example, is a freely permeable surface, which is cheap and easy to install. The path is dug out, levelled and backfilled with either decomposed granite, or hogging and then topped with a layer of gravel or crushed slate. You could also use recycled materials too, such as crushed glass. Another option is pavers or stones which are laid over a bed of sand and gravel so the water can pass through, or flagstones surrounded by gravel.

If the area is going to get a lot of footfall or be used as a driveway, you can use reinforcement grids, which are like a mesh. They are laid in the ground and mesh spaces back filled with gravel or soil and grass seed. Resin is another option for a large expanse, such as a parking area or large drive. Unlike concrete, a resin-bound driveway or path is permeable as well as being non-slip, resistant to weeds and easy to maintain. Resin-bound materials comprise small stones bound together with a high-tech resin. It contains many small gaps, so water can drain away, so it has the appearance of gravel but the durability and permeability of block paving. This is very different from resin-bonded surfacing in which the stones are scattered onto a surface of resin - the result is an impermeable layer.

Slow water with a front garden

Next time you are walking along a typical urban street, have a look at the front gardens. Traditional flower beds and lawns have

more often than not been replaced with hard standing, such as paving or concrete drive for a car. The result of this surfacing, which is impervious to rain, is the considerable run off we see from these urban spaces. Just imagine how much water could be slowed down, if every resident of a street increased the permeability of their front gardens.

It's also easily solved. Cars don't use the central part of the driveway, so it could be replaced with gravel or pavers, both of which allow water to soak away. Equally in the case of a sloped drive a French drain or grate could

Attractive and functional front garden

Left: The steel mesh creates hard standing for a car and allows water to drain away

Water is directed down a slope to a rain garden

be installed at the bottom to collect any water that runs off. Gravel trenches can also be dug along the edge of concrete and paved areas, again to slow down any flow-off and let the water seep safely into the ground.

Build a swale

Swales are brilliant at slowing, storing and spreading water. They simply comprise a shallow trench which carries water safely away from areas at risk of flooding. In fact, a well-positioned swale may be as efficient, if not more so, than a water butt or two. They particularly come into their own in gardens at risk from water flowing in from above. This simple measure can help to distribute the water so it can drain slowly over the garden into areas that need it.

Before you start digging though, remember to watch how water moves through your garden.

Find out where it is coming in from and which route it takes. Also bear in mind swales are suited to shallow slopes of 5–10° or less, any more and you risk the chance of an earth slide during heavy rain. A swale needs to be positioned with the water draining away from any building, edge of a steep slope and from a septic drain. Ideally, it's located uphill from a point where water collects.

To build a swale, dig a trench along a contour line, up to 45cm (18") deep and 61cm (24") wide. Its length depends on how much space you have and how much water needs to be stored. You can work out how much water your roofs and hard surfaces could collect, based on the annual rainfall for your area, so you can see if the capacity of your proposed swale is enough. When you dig the soil from the trench, pile it up on the downhill side to create a berm. Make sure the bottom of the trench is level so that the water lies evenly and doesn't accumulate at one end. Don't fill it immediately but leave the swale empty and watch during the next heavy rainfall.

If the water overflows, the trench needs to be deeper, longer or wider. If a lack of space limits the size of the swale, you can always build a second channel to catch the over-flowing water from the first. Once you are happy with the swale, plant the berm with herbaceous perennials, soft fruit bushes, fruit trees or even hedgerow plants. The roots of these plants will stabilise the berm and their

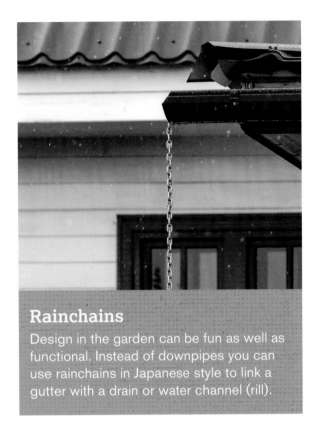

Rainchains
Design in the garden can be fun as well as functional. Instead of downpipes you can use rainchains in Japanese style to link a gutter with a drain or water channel (rill).

leaves will protect the soil. The swale itself can be left empty or backfilled with gravel or mulch. And a final touch is to include an over-spill area to deal with very heavy rain.

If you find your garden experiences heavy run-off and the swale can't cope, lay a porous pipe along the bottom of the channel, which will help to move the water along more quickly and out through the overspill.

GARDENING IN THE SKY

Walking along the 'garden in the sky' on New York's west side is a surreal experience. You are high above the hustle and bustle of the busy city roads enjoying a fabulous prairie planting with views over an iconic waterfront. This is the High Line, an inspirational park built on a disused elevated railway that was used for transporting cattle into New York's meat packing district. It fell into disuse and was about to be demolished before the Friends of the High Line took it over and transformed it into a beautiful public space, a continuous 2.3 km (1.45-mile) long greenway with gardens, art, food stalls and performance areas.

At the start of construction back in 1999, everything was removed from the structure including the rails, although many have been put back in their original position, a drainage system was installed and the structure waterproofed. Once the structure was safe, the landscaping began on soil that ranged in depth from just 45cm (18") to 91cm (36") under trees. One of the landscape designers was Piet Oudolf, famous for his prairie planting style (see page 190). There are more than 500 plant species, including perennials, grasses, shrubs and trees, all chosen for their tolerance of drought and wind hardiness, texture and colour, with a focus on native species. They include: aster, birch, bur oak, catmint, chokecherry, dogwood, echinacea, geum, hydrangea, meadow sage, Michaelmas daisy, milkweed, salvia, sedum, smokebush, Virginia pine, yarrow and winterberry.

Creating a rain garden

A rain garden is just like a sunken bed, positioned carefully to collect run off from surfaces in your outside space. As well as temporarily holding storm water and slowing down run-off from hard surfaces, it has the bonus function of acting as a natural filter for the water running through it. It's stocked with plants that can cope with being flooded on a temporary basis thereby also making an attractive feature out of your useful ally in the battle against flood prevention.

The best place to build your rain garden is several metres away from the house on a flat area or gentle slope (< 10°). This way swales and drainpipes can direct the water into this area where it will collect and slowly drain into the ground (or if sheer volume of rainwater demands, into a further overspill area). As previously mentioned, this should always be situated well away from septic tanks and wells.

Also, do bear in mind that as you'll be relying on your rain garden to allow water to soak away into the ground, it's prudent to check you've chosen the right place (and soil) for such a job. A simple percolation test (see page 67) is therefore recommended before you start construction. You need soil that allows water to drain away at rates of at least 5cm (2") per hour. If percolation rates are slow, you either need to find a different spot or improve the soil with gravel or grit. A rain garden may not suit gardens with heavy clay or a naturally

This decorative granite-sett channel in the path snaking down a slope is a mini-swale, carrying water away from the rest of the garden

Mini-swales

These are shallow trench, backfilled with absorbent material and mulched with bark. A series of mini-swales and swale paths can direct water through your garden and allow it to soak into garden beds. Another advantage of water soaking into the ground, is that you don't get muddy paths with pools of water sitting on the surface.

A small rain garden has been constructed in this suburban garden. (Top) Construction phase

high water table as the water will be too slow draining away. In these cases, a bog garden may be better suited to take advantage of the waterlogged conditions.

These valuable gardens can be any shape, but they do benefit from being as large as possible, so they can effectively deal with an excess of rain in a heavy storm, so with this in mind, its best to aim for 3m (10') wide or more. As a general rule of thumb, the surface area of your rain garden should be at least 10 to 20% of the total area of impermeable surfaces that drain into it, including the roof. If it's too small, it will simply get waterlogged too quickly and overflow.

To construct your rain garden, mark out the boundaries and dig out the soil to a depth of roughly 45cm (1'6"), creating a shallow saucer-shaped depression. Make sure the edges are level and create an earth mound (berm) on the downhill side to hold the water with an overflow zone (which can simply be a notch in the berm that allows excess water to seep away towards a channel or drain). Mix organic matter and grit into the soil and refill the rain garden to the original level.

When it comes to planting, if you imagine that a good root system will hold the soil and take up water, you'll see that the more the merrier is always best. Also, in terms of construction, rain gardens tend to have three growing zones to bear in mind when choosing plants:

- the bottom of the rain garden where there will be the most water and for the longest period
- the sloping sides of the garden which will be wet but for shorter periods of time. Ideally these plants need a good root system to stabilise the slopes
- the upper area which will be the least wet.

It's also good to use a dense and diverse mix of plants so if some fail, others may thrive. Given the damp nature of the bed, avoid any of Mediterranean origin and go for species suited to wet or waterlogged conditions as they have to be able to cope with waterlogging around their roots on a temporary basis.

In the first year you may have to water in dry periods and while the plants are getting established. During this initial period they will be less able to cope with loads of water, so don't allow too much rain to collect there by deepening the overspill area to let more water out. It may also help to place rocks near the entrance to the rain garden to slow down the flow of water and prevent the plants and soil from being washed out.

Another option is a rain garden planter – this is a large container that receives water from a downpipe and which has an overflow pipe leading to the drain. The planter intercepts the rain and holds it back before discharging to the drain, rather like a water butt, but far more attractive. The planter has a deep gravel layer

at the base and is then filled with compost mixed with grit and planted with water-loving plants such as iris, sedges and rush.

Bog gardens

If you have a low-lying area of the garden that is always wet and collects rainwater then maybe it's best to just work with these somewhat soggy conditions, rather than trying to fight against them, through the creation of a bog garden filled with species that love the water. There is always the risk in future that even the bog garden will dry out in a drought so make sure you incorporate plenty of compost or organic matter around planting to enable it to retain moisture.

Green roofs

Green roofs are increasingly common in our cities and they have so many benefits and as we've previously mentioned, the one that interests us the most is the way they help to slow the flow of water off a roof and into the drainage system. They are the start of the sustainable drainage system (SUDS).

These natural, living roofs are beneficial even if our rainfall becomes more intense as they reduce the volume of water hitting the drains at the same time. They also improve stormwater quality and building insulation, reduce the carbon footprint and provide new habitats for wildlife.

A green roof on a log store

In the garden, they can be built on sheds, log stores and even chicken houses. They are relatively simple to install so long as you follow some guidelines, but note that a green roof installed over an occupied building or attached to an occupied building actually requires building regulations.

First, you need to assess the existing roof. The slope is important, no less than 2° and no more than 10°, any steeper you run the risk of the roofing materials slipping, in which case you need to incorporate a grid structure to hold the substrate. Also, you need to work out whether the roof can take the weight! A typical green roof weighs between 60 and 150 kg/m² (12-30.7 psf) when dry and will weigh far more when saturated with water, so make sure it's a sturdy roof with no holes, splits or rotting wood.

A green roof is formed from several layers:

A waterproof and root proof membrane which is laid over the existing asphalt or bitumen layer. This could be a butyl pond liner or a damp-proof membrane.

Containment frame to retain the substrate, made from rot resistant materials, such as treated wood

Rain and cities

When it rains heavily in a city, the abundance of non-water-absorbent hard surfaces often results in a large volume of run off water that the drainage system has to cope with. As storm water from roofs and streets is directed underground and into local water courses, it carries with it debris and contaminants, which then end up in rivers, or eventually the sea. This also means that the urban water table isn't being replenished with clean water but instead is often recharged with such polluted material from storm drains and sewers.

It's no wonder that city planners and land-scape architects are looking to incorporate sustainable drainage features, such as green roofs that retain water and slow down its rate, as well as permeable pavements made using pavers, porous tarmac and pervious concrete which also all offer an ability to put the brakes on the rate of water run off.

In 2009, Toronto passed a by-law that requires all new roof construction and development projects to have green roofs as standard. While, in Canberra, Australia, water is harvested and recycled to help during periods of drought and San Diego's Pure Water Program harvests rainwater with an impressive aim of producing one-third of the city's drinking water through recycling by 2035.

Rain gardens are also appearing in cities as part of soft landscaping schemes, helping to slow down the rate at which water runs off. In Tucson, Arizona rain gardens have been installed along streets to slow, spread and sink water that falls from the sky. Not only does this help during the monsoon rains, but the city looks more attractive and the trees cast shade as a result. In Seattle, homeowners are offered incentives for the construction of rain gardens to aid the city's efforts in slowing down water.

A green roof with a predominantly grass planting

or metal, with drainage outlets to allow water access to the guttering or to drain away. Place a layer of pebbles on the membrane to ensure the drainage system does not get blocked.

Substrate This needs to be lightweight, low in nutrients and moisture retentive, so don't use soil, but lightweight materials such as 75% crushed brick or expanded clay and 25% organic materials such as composted green waste. The depth can range from 70 to 200mm (3 to 8"), the deeper substrate providing greater drought resilience.

Planting You can buy mats of sedum ready to roll out just like a new lawn, or you can direct place plug plants or use seed mixes designed for the dry and windy conditions of the roof top. A diversity of species not only attracts more wildlife, but is more likely to become self-sustaining. When planting, bear in mind that species placed near to the top of the roof are going to experience the driest conditions. But be warned some of the sedums can become a weed problem in the garden, popping up everywhere!

Learning from the past

Walls

The first recorded observations of the benefits of walls date back to 1561 when Conrad Gessner, a Swiss botanist, noted the effects of radiated heat from walls on fruit trees, enabling them to be grown in a more northerly location. During the 1600s the Little Ice Age started to make its presence known and around this time, walls and walled gardens became more important.

This isn't surprising when you consider that a thick wall could raise the temperature of the surrounding air by 10°C (19°F) at night which meant that gardeners in northern England could grow a wide range of frost-sensitive fruits, such as peaches and apricots. By the mid-19th century Montreuil-sous-Bois near Paris had hundreds of kilometres of walls enclosing small spaces (clos) for growing peaches. Dutch gardeners opted for curved walls that were less thick and used fewer materials, but captured more heat and provided extra heat gain, while in eastern England, crinkle-crankie or zigzag walls were more usual. Often walls were topped with overhanging copping stones for added protection, while projecting metal brackets allowed glass, net or canvas to be hung vertically to protect plants.

A crinkle crankle wall requires fewer bricks and traps more heat than a straight wall

The walled gardens of Montreuil-sous-Bois in the 1900s.

A living wall slows down the flow of water

The types of plants that are suitable for these systems depend on the aspect. In sunny positions you could grow strawberries or bedding plants, while a shadier wall would be ideal for salad crops and herbs.

Garden walls

Walls are incredibly useful garden features. In effect they create a localised, protected microclimate and assist in frost avoidance. South and west facing walls are particularly beneficial, taking up heat during the day and releasing it to the benefit of planting nearby. This is useful in spring and autumn, when a boost of just a few degrees can be invaluable. In fact, it is estimated that the presence of a sunny wall is equivalent to moving 5° latitude further south, so the microclimate in a sunny, walled garden in Hampshire or Surrey can be likened to the conditions in Bordeaux.

South facing walls are great for growing heat loving aubergines, peppers and tomatoes plus drought-tolerant Mediterranean plants, as the wall provides heat, shelter and protection from the extremes (especially wind and frost). Do remember it can get very hot too, so water and mulch well. If you are worried about frost sensitive plants in pots, move them beside a wall on a cold night and cover with fleece. You can also construct a temporary lean-to with shelves for trays of sown seeds and young plants and drape fleece or plastic over the front, which should be enough to protect them from frost and heavy rain.

Living walls

In the same way a green roof helps to slow down the flow of water, so can a wall covered by planting. As well as reducing the flow of water to the ground, it can work to improve the aesthetic appearance of the wall, attract wildlife, help to keep a wall cooler in sun and provide extra insulation in winter.

There are small wall planting systems you can buy for gardens, which comprise wall panels or modules filled with light-weight compost, connected to an in-built drip irrigation system.

Right: Sally grows fruit trees along a southwest facing wall while the nearby vegetable beds also benefit from the microclimate created by the high wall.

CHAPTER
SIX

WORKING WITH WILDLIFE
- a natural resilience

What should a garden look like? Although more naturalistically-minded planting has increasingly been seen at flower shows such as RHS Chelsea in recent years, there is still very much an ingrained perception that our outside spaces should be ordered and nature firmly kept in check. The ideal garden from this viewpoint probably has immaculate weed-free, well trimmed short lawns, trees and shrubs uniformly pruned back into place, exceptionally neat, symmetrical flower beds, veg patches full of blocks of produce ... and

all of it managed with meticulous detail for most of the year.

During the summer months, much time is spent primping and pruning to keep everything in its place whilst, at the end of the season as the daylight hours start to shorten, preparation for winter begins in earnest. Old annuals are pulled out, the soil is most likely dug over to expose it to the elements, messy leaf litter is cleared away and all semblance of the natural cycle of decay removed entirely from view.

Left: We need to encourage essential pollinators such as bumble bees

Butterflies are no longer a common sight in gardens

Whilst such a garden might have bird feeders, or a pond, and wildlife will indeed be present, it is essentially a little like another room of the house. Everything is kept in check, almost hoovered clear of dirt and debris, to keep it looking spick-and-span. A garden to be proud of, to show off when family, friends and neighbours come round, because that's the way an outside space should essentially be…pristine and almost clinically clean.

Yet… an awful lot of backbreaking work, the result of keeping an outside space in such a spotless condition also leaves the plants potentially a lot more vulnerable to the elements and needy of year-round attention. As you will have seen by now from the chapter on soil, digging your garden over and leaving it weed-free over winter is damaging, making your precious loam much more susceptible to nutrient loss. Likewise, in the summer months, a neatly ordered and spaced flower bed is going to dry out a lot more quickly than one which is wilder in aesthetic, with much more ground cover to help keep precious moisture in.

A wildlife pond could attract dragonflies

Future pests and diseases - the threat

With milder winters, more pests are able to survive and prosper. For example, for every 1°C (1.8°F) increase in average temperatures, aphids will become active two weeks earlier than usual. Plus, according to scientists in the journal, *Science*, as temperatures rise, so do the metabolic and reproductive rates of insects. On the ground, this means we're facing the prospect of hungrier insects in greater numbers, and there's also the risk of new species moving in and prospering as a result of the changing climate. We'll also see more fungal disease, such as powdery mildew and black spot, and overall there will be an increase in the number of threats to the plants that we grow.

Alongside the many, many timesaving aspects of letting your garden grow a little wilder (removing the need to replenish the lost nutrients from the eroded soil with fertilisers and improvers for one, and reducing the back and forth watering requirements during the summer for another)… the benefits to wildlife are immense. In turn, the advantages to your garden and to you, as the custodian of your plot, are tenfold when it comes to helping to build a natural biodiversity and resilience from within.

The truth of the matter is that building natural biodiversity in your outside space will be a key tactic against the more volatile weather of the climate change future. A much more naturalistic, low maintenance space will be less work for you as the gardener, and will be more able to withstand the vagaries of our future weather.

Letting nature in to lend a helping hand also helps to deal with the increased threat from new and unusual pests that loom on the horizon. A garden that is in balance with nature, and therefore has a wide diversity of plants and animals within it, is a much harder place for individual species to dominate or create problems. Such a biodiverse organic space provides a natural defence that money simply cannot buy, as well as making your garden a truly mesmerising and enticing place in which to be. Imagine being able to spot frogs and newts on the veg patch as you garden, seeing ground beetles and other enthusiastic slug-eating predators in abundance, listening to the sound of bees working the pollen on your plants, watching almost spellbound as a dragonfly comes into view on a warm summer's day.

All creatures have a role to play as part of the natural balance. So, by letting go of this image of the perfect, manicured plot and actively encouraging wildlife in, our workload will be lessened, our gardens afforded greater protection and our lives enriched beyond measure.

Changing seasons

One element of climate change that can't have escaped anyone's notice is the early arrival of spring; we've seen daffodils at Christmas and snowdrops in November. These 'early arrivals' vary, depending on where you are in the world. For every 10 degrees north from the Equator, spring now arrives around four days earlier than 109 years ago and this change is happening at a far faster rate than previously

Snowdrops are appearing ever earlier

thought. In Los Angeles, spring arrives a day earlier than it did in 2008, but in Seattle it's four days earlier and in the Arctic it's 16 days earlier. In 2017, spring in Washington DC was 22 days early. And most worrying of all, one of the most extreme changes is observed in the high Arctic. A further concern is that it's not just that the timings are earlier but that there is far more variability, so one year spring could be incredibly early, and the next be surprisingly late.

These seasonal changes disrupt natural cycles – the migration of birds and amphibians, the

Do you know the beneficial role wasps play?

Yes, they can be the bane of the late summer barbecue, zooming on any sweet-smelling drinks or meaty foods especially, almost as soon as you've laid the picnic table. They also pack a powerful sting if you're unlucky enough to be the recipient of their angry attention. Yet, at that time of year, when they have a well-known reputation for aggressiveness, they are in fact coming to the end of their lifecycle and slowly but surely dying. I think that would make the best of us more than a little grouchy.

Also, it's worth bearing in mind the vital role wasps play in the ecology of your gardens as they are incredibly useful predators, hoovering up aphid infestations on crops and helping to keep greenfly and many types of caterpillar numbers in check on our behalf. Wasps are part of the natural order of predators, keeping other insect numbers in balance. They also play an important role in the pollination of our plants.

pollination of flowers, the availability of food plants for insects and many other ecological relationships. There are other side effects too. Ticks and mosquitoes remain active for longer, the hayfever period goes on and on and plants are at greater risk from frost in spring or from a summer drought.

Changing weather patterns affect insects in a variety of ways, including making it harder for them to find food. Stress will also make them more susceptible to disease, as we see with the spread of varroa mites in honey bee populations. Milder winter or earlier spring can favour pests that come from other parts of world. The spotted-wing drosophila, for example, is now spreading quickly across the UK. One way to help is to grow a wide range of nectar plants with a long season so there is always something for pollinators to find in times of need.

Different creatures you want to encourage onto your plot and how to go about it.

One thing is certain, if you want to improve the climate resilience of your garden, you need more biodiversity, both in the soil (see chapter 4) and above ground. Ultimately, if you allow even one small area of your garden to become a little overgrown, letting wildflowers move in (even in pots), the grass lengthen and a few stinging nettles to prosper and grow, that alone will encourage a greater range of wildlife into your outside space. Add a small pond or water source, a bird feeder or two, some stones or a wood pile, grow a wider range of plants and produce organically, and you will see how your outside space truly comes alive.

Attracting pollinators

We're not just talking about bees either, as many other animals help out in the process of pollinating your plants. From wasps and hoverflies, through to butterflies, moths, flies and even bats, there is actually a larger-than-you-might-think range of creatures that carry out this vitally important role. Here's how to help encourage them in and keep them visiting and thriving in your garden:

Pollen and nectar-rich planting

The greater the mixture of near-year-round flowering planting you have, the better your garden will be from a pollinator perspective. During the summer months, most gardens will have an ample supply of food but having energy-giving nectar on tap early in the season can make all the difference between survival (or not) for bees and other insects that are emerging from hibernation. The same is true

Dandelions are important for early nectar

when it comes to building up supplies to enable insects to overwinter successfully. It will provide them with a greater ability to deal with adverse conditions and fend off disease within their colonies, especially when you consider that honey bees have the ability to self-medicate with plants that are readily available in their vicinity.

Dandelion

For many people, dandelions are the bane of their immaculate lawn. In truth, you don't want these wild flowers setting seed and spreading them far and wide (as they will given half the chance) across your gardens. Yet this plant is built for survival, and its flowers provide a vital source of nectar for bees early in the season when they need it

The flowerheads of Angelica attracts insects

Herbs attract butterflies and other pollinators

most, so letting some grow and flower will provide huge benefit to many of our most vital insects.

Ivy
This plant provides an important late nectar source for overwintering bees, while its berries are a useful food source for birds late in the season.

Honeysuckle
This delicious sweet-scented climber is much-loved by bees and moths.

Snowdrops
These early flowering delights provide another important source of nectar at an otherwise fairly barren time of year.

Hellebores
These pretty winter flowering plants are a real boon for bees.

Gorse and broom
Although you might need a larger garden to accommodate a bush or two, the sweet coco-nut-smelling flowers of gorse (*Ulex*) provide another useful winter source of food. The closely related brooms (*Cytisus* and *Genista*) do well on poor, but well-drained, soils in a sunny aspect and produce masses of fragrant blooms.

Herbs
The likes of lavender, sage, rosemary, thyme, marjoram, chive and mint will draw bees from far and wide to your gardens during the

Allowing brassica to flower early in its second year will attract bees galore

summer months. Beekeepers often recommend these herbs if you're going to grow anything for bees in pots or hanging baskets.

Grow fruit and vegetables

Whilst pollinators are necessary for much of the veg patch, so the veg patch is useful for pollinators. From apple trees and soft fruits, to broadbeans and summer squash, the flowers of our crops are much-favoured sources of nectar and pollen. Allowing some of your brassicas and parsnips, in particular, to overwinter and set flower in their second year is a good way of attracting pollinators and predators to your plot early in the season. The pretty yellow flowers will buzz with pollinator activity. Leek flower heads are also much favoured later in the year. Generally, allowing some of your produce to flower in this way provides a useful source of food for insects, as well as enabling you to save seed.

Habitats

As well as providing food plants, it's also important to help pollinators overwinter successfully on your plot. While honey bees will come from a hive anything up to 5km (3

Frogs are veg patch heroes

Be careful when you mow

During the summer months, amphibians tend to take shelter in long grassy areas so it's important to be vigilant when mowing the lawn. The same goes for moths, as they can often find this an attractive habitat during the day. Leaving some areas of grass to grow long for a number of weeks will afford these beneficial creatures some vital protection.

miles) or so away, bumble bees tend to nest much closer to their food sources. They like to bury themselves into something, such as a dead or decaying branch on a tree, a wood pile, a pile of leaf litter, or in your compost heap. Providing suitable areas for them to find some shelter against the winter elements will enable them to emerge directly where you need them most come early spring.

Amphibians

These delightful creatures are another boon, providing an extremely important service in a myriad of ways. For a start, they will actively hunt out and eat slugs and snails in your garden. As carnivores, they eat whatever they can get their hands (or rather tongues) on, including caterpillars, mosquitos, flies, beetles, spiders, woodlice, ants and, in the case of large toads, sometimes even small mice!

A pond of some form is the most obvious way to attract these creatures. In fact, any water source can be effective when it comes to tempting frogs and toads into your garden (see below). Equally as important, however, is ground cover, both around the pond itself, and along corridors of plants within the garden. These areas provide space for frogs and toads to seek shelter from the midday sun and offer some protection from larger predators, such as cats. Also, it's important not to use any chemical products or pesticides in the garden since amphibians are very sensitive to such toxins.

A compost pile provides an attractive home for amphibians to overwinter (which is why you don't want to turn a heap during the winter months). Another alternative, is a log pile or an old terracotta plant pot raised slightly above the ground to provide vital shelter for toads. A rockery with lots of nooks and crannies to hide behind is another desirable option for frogs. Newts will bury themselves in the ground or find a nice crack in a wall to hide in over winter, so it's important to be especially careful come spring when working the soil. I often come across them buried in the soil in the polytunnels, so I work the soil gently with my hands without digging to ensure they come to no harm. If I were to use a spade to turn the soil, I would be very likely to kill or injure them, so another good reason for not digging soil.

Hedgehogs

The hedgehog is one of our most popular mammals, yet it's in decline. There are far fewer hedgeghogs compared with just 10 years ago. As their natural habitats of woodland edges and hedgerows have declined, gardens have become more important for their survival. These nocturnal visitors truly are the gardener's friend, scoffing slugs, caterpillars, beetles and other invertebrates. They love wild corners where they can find somewhere to rest, nest and hibernate. Log piles, compost heaps and heaps of leaves all provide a warm, overwintering spot. A hedgehog travels several kilometres every night in search for food, so it's vital that our gardens have an entry/ exit point for them. This just needs to be is a 13x13cm (5x5") gap under the fence or wall, linking your garden with your neighbour's to create a hedgehog highway.

The hedgehog is a true friend of the gardener

Birds

It's impossible to imagine a garden without a varied assortment of feathered friends. As well as making our outdoor spaces so much more enjoyable, they also act as useful allies in the garden, picking up and eating troublesome pests, such as slugs, snails, aphids and caterpillars. Feeders and a water source will, of course, attract birds, but it's also important to think about plants which will provide more food and places to shelter. Leaving seed heads in place over winter benefits birds, as much as the soil, while hedging plants such as hawthorn, and wall plants, like ivy, also provide a source of berry-powered winter fuel as well as a nighttime roost in winter.

Building a bug hotel

One way to ensure a variety of minibeast habitats is to build a bug hotel from old pallets, bits of wood, old bamboo canes, bricks, clay pipes and pots, and anything else you can find. The nooks and crannies are the perfect hiding places for insects, spiders, centipedes and even amphibians. The more varied the habitats you create the more biodiversity you will attract. Use old pallets to create layers (floors) and then fill the gaps with your recycled materials, the more varied the materials the better. You can finish off with a roof or even create a green roof (see page 93).

Encouraging predators

Many animals in the garden have a valuable role as a predator, helping to keep some of the pests in check. Look no further than ladybirds, hoverflies and lacewings. This fantastic trio produce larvae that will hoover their way through aphids like there is no tomorrow. They all provide a vital role in keeping pest numbers in check.

Ladybirds and lacewings will also eat red spider mite, while hoverflies play an important role in plant pollination. Plants to entice them in include stinging nettles (a small quantity at the back of a garden) and fennel. In fact, one organic veg producer always picks a large bunch of fennel and takes it into one of his polytunnels if he's had an aphid outbreak to allow the ladybird larvae to work their magic.

Parasitic wasps will also be drawn to fennel. These valuable wasps lay their eggs in the body of caterpillars (yuk!). When they hatch, the wasp larvae literally eat the caterpillars from the inside. Then they pupate and emerge as new wasps.

Other essential predators in the garden include spiders and ground beetles. You may jump back when you lift a pot and a black beetle scuttles away, but this fast-moving insect is a voracious predator, chasing down prey on its long legs.

Build your own wildlife pond

Wherever you live, whether it's in the bustling heart of a city or the quiet countryside, if you create a water source outside then you're almost guaranteed to draw wildlife in. Even the smallest water feature can attract a wide range of beneficial creatures to help provide a source of interest and wonder, as well as making sure your garden truly comes alive.

There's nothing like listening to bird song as you sit or work outside, and such feathered friends will soon be drawn to any opportunity for a little drink or splash around in water that you make available to them. In return for refreshments, they'll most likely reward you by dealing with slugs, snails, or aphids that they happen to find causing trouble on your nearby plants. Much like other water-loving creatures, such as frogs, toads, newts, hedgehogs and dragonflies, birds provide a very useful and equally mesmerising addition to any outside space.

Building the pond

The first step is to find a suitable liner, preformed plastic pond or a container. If you opt for a pond liner, there is a huge range of butyl rubber liners available nowadays in a wide range of sizes, and they are very easy to work with. Choose an area with sunlight but also some daytime shade. To make it tempting to as much wildlife as possible, some privacy is preferable, so siting it in a corner or at the back of your garden would be ideal.

It's perfectly feasible to have a raised water feature. For a raised patio pond, positioning doesn't matter so much; any water source is beneficial so just choose where it would fit in best, nestled somewhere on your balcony or allotment for example. However, amphibians will struggle to get in and out of a raised pond, so it is always preferable to have a pond that is sunk into the ground. To do this you will have to dig a big hole in your chosen spot. You could meticulously measure the area first, or just figure it out as you go along; you'll get there either way. Ideally you want the container sitting either just below or level to the ground around it.

It's important to provide access for wildlife, and you can do this using some of the natural materials you have to hand. The aim is to make it easy for frogs, toads and newts, in particular, to get in and out. Pebbles, placed in and around the pond will do the trick nicely, and have the added benefit of providing places under which to hide. Planting around the area also provides welcome ground cover, and will work to make the space even more amphibian-friendly. Plus, if you carefully position stones, rocks or wood in the pond to allow for shallow edges, this makes it easier for the likes of birds and hedgehogs to bathe.

It's best to fill your pond with rainwater, as tap water is chlorinated, so the contents of a water butt would be ideal. Otherwise you can just leave it to fill naturally over time.

You can help keep the pond in good health (and clear) with the addition of aquatic plants, such as pondweed. These will help to aerate the pond and be a good source of food for the pond life. If the water level dips over time, simply keep it topped up with rainwater again.

Create a pond and watch the wildlife move in

New visitors

As the water settles, birds are likely to move in first, enjoying the opportunity for a drink and maybe even a bath. Over time, as the pond matures, you're likely to see pond skaters, backswimmers and diving beetles. Frogs and newts take up residence in even the smallest of ponds, especially if they have ground cover nearby.

[Build your own wildlife pond was first published in *The Primrose Water Feature Book* by Kim Stoddart and published by Primrose]

CHAPTER
SEVEN

THE VEG PATCH

We live in very uncertain times, and food security in the future is going to be impacted dramatically by the changing climate. As consumers reliant on buying in all their food for the table, this leaves us open to the volatility of what is a global commodity market. A flood or drought in one part of the world, decimating harvests of certain produce can have a dramatic knock-on impact on supply and prices in the UK and elsewhere. The same goes for demand. For example, in the prolonged heatwave of 2018, when demand for summer salad soared, veg growers struggled to keep up as lettuce simply stops growing in temperatures above 30ºC. The only available sources were overseas and so, as imports increased, so did prices.

Our changing climate is most likely to make food shortages, supply chain delays and soaring costs a distinct part of our future. When you consider this alongside the undeniable fact that out-of-season shop bought produce is often a sorry excuse for freshly picked sweetness, the case for growing your own is rock solid. There's no plastic packing, no shipping or haulage and no unknown chemicals to worry about, just a great feeling as you consume the veg you have lovingly grown. It is well worthwhile on many levels and there is yet another benefit. If you improve the resilience of your garden to extreme weather events and the threat of new pests and diseases, you will be rewarded with the ability to grow a greater variety of plants and vegetables all year round.

Left: A biodiverse planting on Kim's veg patch

Change is in the air

Many of our current grow-your-own practices are high maintenance and vulnerable to the elements, based as they are around a set of (let's face it) rather exacting do's and dont's when it comes to the cultivation of home-grown fruit and vegetables.

A lot of this comes down to an ingrained desire for uniformity – be it straight lines or blocks and blocks of produce that you see when you travel to any allotment around the UK. We're programmed to keep our veg plots looking very neat and tidy, to keep nature very much in its place and under control. Yet, as you will have read in the previous chapter on wildlife, actually letting nature in to lend a helping hand makes for a much hardier, low maintenance, productive and, arguably, more enjoyable place in which to grow. It encourages the natural biodiversity in nature. It means the difference between managing a plot that is truly alive, in which plants, the soil and the creatures all work in balance together, and a sterile, high maintenance plot, which has exacting demands because it's kept so clinically clean.

Understandably, jumping wholeheartedly into a different way of gardening and growing food may be too much for some people to take on all at once. Yet shoring up your defences, even little by little, will enable you to weather the extremes that we face in the future.

Creating a more resilient garden means, in part, becoming a more resilient gardener. The two go hand in hand, and that will take time and confidence. It's really not rocket science, just an ability to look outside of the traditional gardening rulebooks and, instead, to tune in to one's self-instinct, as well as the natural potential of your outside space.

When to grow

With increasingly changeable weather, we can no longer predict when to grow plants based on a 'standard timetable'. Although many gardeners take undoubted comfort from certain crops being sown, regular as clockwork, at a certain time of year, such a disconnected approach is becoming increasingly unreliable. Nowadays, it's vital to look at what is happening around us, at what the weather is doing, and to adopt a more flexible approach so that 'good old common sense' dictates when will be the best time to sow your precious seed.

It's worth changing these patterns of planting anyway, as the ability to adapt, to swap and change where needed be will be key. Ultimately, we're looking at a future where both early and late sowings are likely to be possible, as we move towards a two-season pattern of growth, with spring to early summer and late summer to autumn, which is more typical of the Mediterranean.

Learning from the past

Medieval gardens - organic by design

Medieval gardens were rarely decorative. Instead, they served a purely functional use, especially for those in so-called lower status positions, as they were used to provide food for the table. Within this system (and the growing of edibles), some weeds were actively encouraged because of their many uses in the home. As well as protecting the ground against nutrient leaching over winter, many weeds that we would nowadays remove, such as chickweed, fat hen and ox tongue, would have been encouraged to self-seed and grow in-between crops. This would have served the purpose of attracting beneficial insects to aid natural pest control, as well as helping to provide a welcome food source, especially come the 'hungry gap' in spring. Ground was always kept covered with plants, helping to keep moisture in during the warmer months and avoiding erosion over winter.

Herbs also played a very important role, with a wide range being grown for a myriad of practical uses; from flavouring food in the kitchen, to use in beds and bedding (wormwood et al), to keeping out bed bugs, for dyeing, to ward off evil spirits (rosemary), and also for a range of medicinal purposes (such as comfrey to help mend broken bones). Seed-saving was also an important part of the gardening calendar, with plants harvested at the end of the season to provide the source of planting for future years.

Flowers were only grown in the highest status gardens at first, with plant finders often sponsored by wealthy gardeners to seek and find interesting species to be weaved into the planting on their estates back home. It was only over time that these species would have filtered down to more everyday use in less prestigious gardens.

Although most medieval gardens followed a three-year rotation system of peas and beans, followed by grain and then a fallow period, a number of crop seeds were often sown together to reduce risk of failure. This would have resulted in a mixed planting which, combined with the ample wildflowers and weeds grown alongside, would have created a healthy degree of biodiversity and natural resilience.

Building resilience in the gardener - a change in mindset

This book gives lots of advice, information and ideas for you to protect and prepare your garden (and the plants therein) for the climate change extremes of weather ahead.

We have already established that it's no longer 'gardening as usual' and, whilst this undoubtedly presents challenges, it also offers great opportunities. There's no turning back the clock and the development of a personal hardiness inside better enables us to deal with the hostilities on the outside.

What might help in this process of adapting to new ways of gardening is the knowledge that, actually, much of what we consider traditional advice nowadays is based on the comparatively recent practices of Victorian country houses. In those days, activities and the calendar were designed for a team of gardeners working at the behest of the lord or lady of the manor. Everything was designed to keep the gardens primped and polished, and the kitchen full of produce, for their master's pleasure.

Also, there was the not insignificant matter of keeping the staff busy all year round, so there was no slacking off. As such, work generation was certainly part of the equation at quieter times of year with the creation of time-consuming practices which are still dutifully carried forth to this day.

Prior to this very controlled Victorian approach, in which outside spaces were kept meticulously tidy, the gardens of everyday, working folk (aka peasants), exhibited a more free-spirited, practically-minded ethos. Their gardens had a much more 'higgeldy piggeldy' planting of crops and flowers and weeds, many of which were important for both their culinary and medicinal uses in the home.

More resilient produce on the veg patch

Perennial veg are incredibly useful plants and are another climate change 'must have', as their longevity enables them to stand firm relatively easily against more challenging conditions. With their deeper root structure, they are able to seek out moisture more effectively during a dry period and absorb an excess of rainwater, to the benefit of the plants around them, during storms.

The fact that the soil in which they grow remains undisturbed also provides benefit in a number of exciting ways that we don't yet fully understand. It is the amazing underground world, with its complex fungal and microbial activity, that is so essential for health and vitality above ground.

Some of the most commonly used perennials for the veg garden	
Asparagus (*Asparagus officinalis*)	Easily grown from seed or planted on from bought-in crowns, this delicious perennial will, when established, keep on providing for many more seasons. So, being patient until you can take your first harvest in the third year will be paid back with plentiful returns for many years thereafter. These plants just require a nutrient-rich, pervasive weed-free patch of ground as their long term home.
Cardoon (*Cynara cardunculus*) and **globe artichoke** (*Cynara cardunculus* Scolymus Group)	These thistle-like, highly ornamental plants will reliably return each year with just a little care. In the case of globe artichoke, the heads themselves are edible, while with cardoon it's the blanching stalks that are highly prized in the kitchen.
Jerusalem artichoke (*Helianthus tuberosus*)	This rich, nutty tuber fits in well to the climate change garden. It's tall growing stems can provide a useful barrier on the veg patch against wind to the benefit of your plot overall. It will cast shade, so that's worth bearing in mind, but otherwise these tasty tubers can be harvested in late autumn/early winter onwards. You don't need to worry about leaving some in the ground to grow on the following season because it will happen whether you mean to or not! These plants have a strong survival instinct, and produce tubers deep in the ground, so new plants can always be expected to emerge with gusto in the spring.
Oca (*Oxalis tuberosa*)	These highly colourful small South American tubers are becoming more readily available to buy, thanks in big part to www.ocabreeder.org and their work championing the growing of this nutritious plant in the UK.
Perennial kale (*Brassica oleracea* Ramosa Group)	Daubenton's and Taunton Deane Kale are two of the most commonly known varieties of perennial kales, which will reliably stand firm for many years. These plants, also known as cottager's kale, would have been common in vegetable gardens up until Victorian times. They are damaged by caterpillars in the same way as other brassica but, being perennial, they have the resilience to bounce back as if nothing has happened.
Rhubarb (*Rheum x hybridum*)	It may not be glamorous, but this stalwart fruit is very weather hardy and reliable. It will reappear like clockwork each spring, year after year once fully established, and can handle regular pickings. Once a plant gets really big, it's crown will just need dividing (cutting in half with a spade) providing you with another rhubarb plant (or cut in half again), to be planted out elsewhere on your patch.

Some of the most commonly used perennials for the veg garden	
Sea kale (*Crambe maritima*)	Found wild on coastal shingle banks, it is traditionally forced in winter for its white stems, but the leaves and flower spikes can be harvested too.
Skirret (*Sium sisarum*)	This root crop was popular in the Middle Ages for its thin roots that taste of carrots and parsnip. Harvested all year.
Sorrel (Rumex)	This zesty leaf provides a valuable addition to any veg patch. Its leaves are delicious in any number of dishes, and it requires little to no care whatsoever.
Walking/tree onions (*Allium cepa* Proliferum Group)	This variety of onion will (as the name suggests) gradually 'walk' around your veg patch as it produces bulbs on the end of the foliage which eventually bend over and plant themselves in the surrounding soil.

Herbs - a place in thyme

Herbs have a valuable role to play in the more environmentally-minded garden, attracting pollinators and beneficial insects, as well as furnishing us with very healthy, flavoursome material for the kitchen. Of the many herb varieties there are to grow, the perennials make an especially useful addition. As well as being incredibly low maintenance, they will also help to protect soil against erosion over winter, providing structure as their roots bind the soil particles together for better absorption of rain.

Mixed planting or rotation

Look at most veg patches or allotments around the UK and you will see patch upon patch of block planted vegetables. This is what we've been led to believe growing fruit and vegetables should look like. Equally, the mentality of 'grow it, harvest, then pull it out' has been ingrained in much traditional gardening advice over the years. It's all very much built around this idea of keeping nature in check, with produce positioned in neat, weed-free lines for the designated growing season.

Although in an organic system, a process of crop rotation is recommended (to ensure that the soil isn't drained of vital nutrients at the end of each season and disease does not build up), it doesn't have to be this way all the time. Growing varieties of crop in an ordered succession (with brassicas following legumes, following potatoes and so forth) will ensure order and overall soil health and fertility. However, if you plant different types of vegetable and even fruit, all mixed in together in your bed then the soil doesn't get depleted in the same way it would with mono block planting. Instead, because you have fast-growing crops,

Sally's perennial bed with (L to R) sweet cicely, Chinese artichoke, sea kale and Good King Henry

such as lettuce, growing alongside a hungrier tomato plant, with a few Mediterranean herbs, pea plants, a few cabbages and lots of nasturtium, carrots, some onions and maybe some radishes, there is a natural biodiversity that enables you to ignore the crop rotation system entirely.

The key is just to ensure that there is sufficient space between hungrier plants, and balance between the crops which are planted together. The key is not to have too many of one type in a particular area, to ensure the soil retains fertility and pest build-up doesn't become an issue.

In fact, this more free-spirited method of growing can also help to keep pest numbers in check. If you consider that it's often recommended to companion plant calendula or onions around carrots to help prevent carrot root fly attack, just imagine this principle on a much larger scale. It's essentially harder for a particular pest problem to get out of control

Lowering your carbon footprint - working with waste

In this rather crazy, materialistic world in which we live, and in which our reliance on disposable materials, especially plastics, has become a blight on the natural environment, finding productive ways to use such waste creates brownie points all-round. It also helps to build confidence and develop the skills necessary to think on your feet, to get creative, and come up with ideas and solutions of how to use readily available materials on your own plot.

Using plastic bottles as cloches
Don't throw away plastic bottles. By cutting the bottom off a plastic bottle, the remaining plastic can be used as a protective cover for potted seedlings to help them on their way. Keeping the lid off enables some air to circulate, so the well-insulated young plant is able to thrive and grow in its plastic bubble. Such cut-down bottles can also be stored away at the end of the growing season and used over and over again, before eventually being added to the recycling.

Planting trays and pots
So many plastic pots from newly bought plants end up being ditched, yet they can often be successfully used repeatedly for many years to come. If they crack around the edge, then gaffer tape or similar can be used to provide a repair. If we can abandon our 'use once and throw away mentality', and treat plastics that have already been created as a potentially useful item with a long term purpose, then that will be an important part of the solution. Of course, we should still look at more environmentally friendly alternatives. In the same vein, plastic fruit and vegetable containers and yoghurt or food pots from the kitchen can be re-used for planting seedlings. Even cardboard toilet roll inners can be used as a biodegradeable seedling pot.

Cardboard and kitchen waste into the compost

Compost plays a vital role in ensuring, the continued fertility of your veg patch. A huge amount of kitchen waste, including cardboard, can also be successfully composted, dramatically reducing the amount of direct waste that goes to landfill.

Old carpets
An old wool carpet is perfect for covering soil in winter and killing weeds

Getting inventive with salvage
It's staggering and appalling in equal measure how much waste we send to landfill each year. If we can start to see these materials, which are so casually disposed of, as a valuable resource for the future, the less disposable our world as a whole will become. It's really easy and incredibly rewarding to find a valuable use for the sorts of items that would most frequently end up in a builder's skip.

An old carpet protects the soil through winter

Old guttering repurposed as the perfect seed tray

Tips for veg growing in a hot summers

Growing vegetables in a dry, hot summer can be challenging, as gardeners certainly found out in 2018. With threats of hose pipe bans, and dwindling supplies in water butts and tanks, keeping beds watered was difficult and, in some cases, costly due to water metering charges. But with careful planning you can grow a wide range of veg successfully.

Mulching will help your soil to retain as much moisture as possible, and if you combine that with a no-dig approach and raised, or mound beds, you will be well on the way to success.

Shade Intense sun can damage young plants, for there are only so many cycles of wilting and rehydrating that leaves can take without dying. As well as mulching, design your veg plots to make best use of natural shade and make sure you have enough space to erect shade nets. Taller crops can be planted to cast shade over more susceptible ones. For example, a row of sunflowers casts a light dappled shade and also reduces wind speed. Often gardeners pop a mesh cover over brassicas to stop butterfly and bird damage, and, as well as protecting the crop, it casts shade, helping to reduce the temperature overall.

Sow and plant early Spring sowings and plantings are likely to be able to get established before the onset of hot weather

when there isn't such a huge source of food in one place for them to get excited about. Instead, they have to hunt harder to find their target of opportunity, so this provides another tick in the resilience box.

These techniques become increasingly important when you consider that, with our changing climate, we are going to have to deal with a much broader range of pests and diseases than ever before.

Grow lettuce between other crops and pick early

Sprawling nasturtiums shade the soil

and the drying out of soil. Later sowings and plantings are more likely to fail due to heat, so the ground needs to be watered well, although a really late sowing may be able to grow on through autumn.

Salad crops Their leafy shoots, with high water content and shallow roots, mean that these crops are more vulnerable to water stress and they need watering, so grow them in a small space and pick early. Lettuce, though, does bolt if stressed.

Grow more early crops If dry summers become the norm, then think about crops that complete their growth before the heat of summer sets in, such as overwintered broad beans, onion sets, early peas and preserve the harvest for use later in the summer.

Use ground cover in-between plants Light-on-the-soil crops, such as salad leaves, make very good fillers around hungrier crops, helping to cast shade onto the soil and preventing it drying out too quickly. The leaves of sprawling plants, such as squash, can also be useful in the same way. Other good ground cover plants include oca, summer herbs and nasturtium.

Getting seeds to germinate

Ensuring successful germination in warm weather is tricky, especially with lettuce, so water the drill several times before you sow to raise the moisture level of the soil. The water cools the soil too. Sow the seeds, cover lightly with soil, and don't water again until germination has taken place. It can help to rig up

Learning from the past

Heritage veg

Kitchen gardens of the past lacked hose pipes and gardeners had to rely on saving water in the garden or lugging it by bucket. Heritage veg may be the answer in the future. Look for slower growing, deep rooted varieties. They may not yield as much but will be more resilient to a hot, dry summer. For example, heritage runner beans have much deeper roots than the modern varieties selected for high yields and rapid time to harvest .

Beetroot can cope with dry summers

some shade to protect the seedlings from the sun's heat and to reduce evaporation from the soil.

How will veg crops cope in the climate change garden?

Beetroot These plants have surprisingly deep roots. They can be sown early and late to take advantage of the longer growing season. They don't need watering as it encourages leafy growth but the soil must not be bone dry. Keep thinning the last sowing, so the last few have plenty of space to expand, and pull soil up around the roots to protect from frost and snow.

Brassica Modern varieties tend to have shallow roots, so a dwarf variety means dwarf roots too. In general, opt for the larger, traditional varieties that produce deeper roots and mulch well. Many of the brassica, especially kales, can be started early when the soil has plenty of moisture so their roots are established before a summer drought.

Kale, Brussels sprouts and sprouting broccoli don't need much water unless there is a long period of drought. Without water their growth will be slow and the plants can look quite sad by the end of summer, but they pick up when the rain returns and will grow on

Brassicas vary in their tolerance to drought

The leafy growth of leeks shades the soil

through autumn into winter.

Calabrese needs moisture to produce flower shoots and stay tender, so is least suited to a dry summer. Opt for early varieties or an alternative, such as the tasty broccoli raab or overwintering sprouting broccoli. Summer cabbage and kohlrabi are very sensitive to drought too.

Carrot Juicy varieties such as Nantes have less fibrous roots, which means the roots are more likely to split early in dry conditions, but the advice is not to water as it lowers yield. Variety selection will become increasingly important.

Celery and celeriac Both these crops are susceptible to drought so need watering.

Chard Despite its large leaf area, chard is pretty tolerant of dry conditions and can be likened to beetroots in its water needs.

Jerusalem artichoke This crop has deep roots so there is no need to water it. In fact, too much water can encourage leaf growth rather than tubers.

Leek Many have found that leeks survive dry conditions well, but they do need a moisture retentive soil. They grow slowly but pick up

Some varieties of lettuce are more drought resilient than others

THE **CLIMATE CHANGE** GARDEN

again in autumn. It may be wise to opt for vigorous varieties that mature later in the year when there is more rain around.

Legumes In the drought of 2018 it was clear that runner beans suffered more than French beans, and more exotic choices such as chickpeas, lentils and butterbeans thrived.

Broad beans and fava beans can be sown in autumn to get an early start and complete their life cycle before the summer heat sets in. Early varieties of peas may come into their own as they too can complete their growth and fruiting before the dry weather kicks in, but second and third sowings may have lower yields in dry weather. With runner beans, make sure they have plenty of organic matter in the soil. Ideally, backfill a trench with organic matter and mulch the plants well. Watering is particularly important at the start of flowering and during pod formation.

Lettuce This is a cool weather crop and many varieties just go to seed in hot, dry summers. Also, they fail to germinate when temperatures rise above 21°C. A leafy type may be more resilient, especially oakleaf lettuce, which has proved to be very resilient to high temperatures and lack of water, plus it can survive light frosts. You can reduce the heat burden on lettuce by planting it in the shadow of taller plants or by shading the bed.

Onion These are established in spring so there should be moisture in the ground, but

Presprouting seeds

Presprouting seeds is a technique used by growers in dry areas to save water and ensure successful germination. Simply soak seeds overnight, drain them, then leave in a dish. Rinse and drain once or twice a day until the first roots appear, at which point they are ready for sowing. To make it easier to sow them use a fluid drilling method. This involves mixing the seeds into a starch gel to help disperse the seeds through the drill. It's simply a couple of tablespoons of cornflour mixed into a pint of boiling water, which is left to cool and form a gel. The seeds are mixed gently into the gel and tipped into a plastic bag. When you are ready to sow the seeds, cut off the corner of the bag (like an icing bag) to create a small hole through which to squeeze the gel into the drill (it's wise to practice this with old seed first). Using this method ensures the seeds are surrounded by a gel and are not water stressed. Plants will appear quickly too as they are pre-germinated.

a dry spring means water will be needed for good establishment. Don't water after mid-July as this will delay ripening.

Parsnip This is a deep-rooted crop so there is no need to water.

Sweet tomatoes

James Wong recommends spraying a dilute solution of soluble aspirin (half a tablet in one litre of water) over your tomato plants to boost the sugar content of the fruits. Aspirin resembles salicylic acid, a plant stress hormone, so aspirin tricks the plant into thinking it's under stress and it sends more sugar to its fruits, and you get sweeter tomatoes. But just as importantly, it boosts the plant's resistance to cold, drought, heat stress and late blight. Try it next time!

Another plus is that tomatoes grown with less water tend to be tastier as there is less watering down of flavour!

Potatoes Coming from the Andes, potatoes are more tolerant of dry summers than many other veg. There is a wide choice of varieties, but the more resilient types are those that are very late and slow maturing and that can be lifted in autumn after they have time to recover from any drought. The advantage of a drier summer is less blight. It's vital to ensure sufficient water during the early stages of tuber initiation and around flowering.

Radicchio This originates from the alpine regions of northern Italy and is hardy. It is sown later in the year and harvested from November to April. In fact, it needs cold for its leaves to turn red, so a mild winter may produce less coloured radicchio. With this crop it's important not to sow too early, otherwise you end up with a green lettuce that's hairy and bitter, so make sure you sow in the heat of summer and let it grow through the cold weather.

Spinach A leafy plant that needs watering, but it can survive wet winter weather

Swede and turnip These have deep roots, like beets, and can continue to grow through drought. Plants from a late sowing will struggle through a dry summer and appear stunted, but they have the capacity to recover and grow into decent sized roots by early winter.

Sweetcorn plants have a poor root system

Squash leaves shade the ground

Summer squash, courgette and winter squash It's best to sow these in modules as they need the right soil temperature to germinate. To get good growth, plant on a mound of compost to provide moisture retention and fertility. They wilt in hot weather, with some varieties being more prone to heat than others, but they recover. However, wilting may indicate that they are planted too close together and are not getting enough water from the available root zone. There are some newer compact varieties, but their weaker root systems mean they are less able to cope with drought. Summer squash, such as yellow crookneck, are particularly drought tolerant

and high yielding as their large leaves help to shade the soil and keep temperatures down, but courgettes and marrows need a rich soil with plenty of moisture holding capacity and will require regular watering. You could start them earlier, planting them out under a cloche or even in a tyre with a sheet of Perspex across the top for frost protection. A tyre will shade the roots later in the season too.

Sweetcorn This water demanding crop often has poorly developed roots and requires watering. You could opt for some of the more drought-hardy field corns, but choose your variety carefully as many are bred for making flour and other uses.

Tomato This crop loves the heat and a longer growing season suits them well. When planting, trim the lower leaves and place deep in the ground so that leaf scars are covered by the soil and will sprout roots. Their roots are mycorrhizal, so can be dusted with mycorrhizal powder to boost early water and nutrient uptake.

If you have plenty of space you may want to think about growing the crop without support, in its natural form as a sprawling vine that covers the ground. This habit shades the roots, allows the stems to root and draw nutrients from a further point in the ground, but harvesting fruits is not so easy.

Especially drought-resistant varieties include Roma, San Marzano, black crim, early girl (cool tolerant so gets an early start), sweet million, sungold and other cherry varieties. The darker pigmentation of the chocolate and black tomatoes blocks the sun's rays rather like a sun screen, preventing sun scald and reducing water demand. Tomato 'Principe Borghese' can be sown early for a crop in early summer and then sown again for an autumn crop.

Growing tomatoes under cover in hot weather can be problematic due to the extreme heat and high humidity experienced in polytunnels during the height of summer. This can adversely affect pollination which, combined with fewer pollinators flying to assist the

Chickpeas love warm, dry summers

pollination of tomato flowers (which are self-fertile but are boosted by pollinators), may mean a poor harvest. For a polytunnel crop, choose varieties that flower early and reach picking stage sooner and look for disease resistance as late blight spreads more readily in hot and humid conditions.

Some vegetables to try

As our summers get warmer and the growing season lengthens, there are a number of more unusual vegetables well worth trying:

Edamame beans are an easy-to-grow crop

Edamame or soybeans (*Glycine max*) A bush bean that needs a long growing season. Plant the seedlings in a well-drained soil in a sunny position either after the risk of frost has passed, or earlier under fleece. If you want edamame beans, pick the pods while they are still green. The easiest way to remove the beans from the pod is to boil them so the beans slip out. If you want soybeans, leave the pods on the plant to ripen and turn brown.

Butter beans or lima beans (*Phaseolus lunatus*) Runner beans suffer in a dry summer, so you might want to try growing butter beans instead. Grown in the same way, they positively enjoy the heat. They produce short pods with two or three fat white seeds, which can be dried and used in soups.

Cowpeas or black-eyed peas (*Vigna unguiculata*) are grown in the southern USA, Africa and Asia. It's an easy to grow, warm weather crop. The peas will tolerate heat and drought. The pods are picked and boiled or stir-fried.

Okra (*Abelmoschus esculentus*) A heat-loving crop, originally from Africa, but now grown across the world. It comes in lots of different varieties, so you need to find one that will suit your conditions.

Tomatillo (*Physalis ixocarpa*) This is the savoury version of the cape gooseberry and it can be used in salsa and sauces. It scrambles over the ground and is slow to mature. As the

Huauzontle (*Chenopodium berlandieri*) This tall plant is a relative of quinoa. The edible leaves are green with pink stripes. It's drought resistant and the pink seeds can be saved and used to make tortilla. It grows fast, so can be sown in late summer.

Chickpea (*Cicer arietinum*) This legume needs a long season. It's frost sensitive, so the young plants are transplanted after the last frosts or protected by cloche or fleece. The pods contain one or two seeds that can be harvested green or left to dry.

Kim picks produce all year round in her tunnel

fruit ripens, the husk peels back to reveal a green or violet coloured fruit. They need a long summer to mature, but can be prolific.

Yardlong beans (*Vigna sesquipedalis*) These are tropical beans and, as the name suggests, the plant produces long, thin beans. It's usually grown in a polytunnel, but will do well outside planted along a south-facing wall.

Growing under cover

Having the ability to cover your plants, should the need arise, will be invaluable in the face of volatile weather, especially early and late in the year. Cover will provide protection for your more fragile seedlings and enable those frost-sensitive plants to grow for a few weeks longer. It enables you to tap into a much

longer growing season, as well as providing a safety net against the worst of the extreme weather of the future.

There are many ways to go about providing cover, from the installation of a polytunnel or greenhouse, to the use of protective covers and structures, which provide many of the same benefits, just on a smaller scale. No matter your budget or site, there are a range of solutions that can assist your food-growing efforts.

A densely planted polytunnel bed with French marigolds to attract pollinators

Polytunnel growing

These vital covered structures are increasing in popularity, as they enable the 'grow your own' enthusiast to greatly extend the range of edibles that they can grow in new and exciting ways. From reliable crops of tomatoes, cucumbers, aubergines, peppers and chillies to sweet potatoes, melons and grapes, all these fruits and vegetables will thrive under cover in all corners of the UK. In addition,

tunnels also provide an undercover outside space that can be used by the gardener on even the wettest of days, so it will double as an attractive and protective haven in which to sit and ponder your climate change gardening day ahead.

Polytunnels are a lot cheaper to buy than greenhouses and relatively straightforward (with a little help from a few friends) to put up. If you can find the space, they really will take crop-growing to a new level and allow

Spring in Kim's polytunnel

you lots of room for experimentation. As well as enabling you to widen the range of fruit and vegetables that can be grown, they also enable you to overwinter many more plants successfully, and to save seed from a greater diversity of plants than would be possible in an outdoor space.

Where to locate your tunnel

Generally speaking, planning permission is not required for a polytunnel if the structure is less than three metres tall and doesn't take up more than half of your garden. It also shouldn't be positioned too close to a road, or in such a way as to cause offence to a neighbour by blocking out light, or being too visible from their garden.

Increasingly, allotment committees are becoming more receptive to the idea, although most tend to favour structures at the much smaller end of the scale. But, wherever you live, it's wise to check first with your local planning authority.

From an installation perspective, you will need to find a sunny spot that is as level as possible. Positioning the polytunnel with a north-to-south orientation has generally been recommended in the past, as that enables you to get the most sun possible during the day. However, with more periods of extreme sunshine on the horizon (as in 2018), it's worth thinking about a position that affords some shade for part of the day. East-to-west positioning, therefore, may be more suitable.

Nearby hedging or trees would be beneficial in terms of early morning or late afternoon shading, so the tunnel doesn't heat up quite as much in the peak of summer. Hedging can also reduce wind speeds (see Chapter 3) as well as helping to screen your polytunnel, enabling it to blend better into its surroundings. Trees and shrubs will also help to soak up excess water running off the polytunnel and minimise waterlogging in and around your plot, making a valuable contribution to your climate change garden.

Making your plastic last longer

The polytunnel structure has the potential to last a very long time (decades in fact), it's the plastic cover that requires replacement more often. Manufacturers recommend every four years as (over time) UV light causes the plastic to become brittle and less visible light can pass through so the tunnel becomes less and less effective as a growing space. That said, one of Kim's tunnels lasted 10 years with the same plastic cover, so when your structure is well cared for, the plastic may last much longer than the recommended guidelines.

Cleaning Keeping the plastic clean and free of algae, fungi and debris, such as fallen leaves, is very important, as such materials will erode the plastic over time. Cleaning the plastic and keeping the tunnel clear is a vital job in the polytunnel gardening calendar.

A hand-held sprinkler is effective but time consuming

Ventilation

If you ever hear someone referring to poly-tunnel growing as being hard or tricky (which it absolutely isn't), airflow is probably the main reason why. Ensuring sufficient airflow is incredibly important to the health and vitality of the ecosystem within your tunnel.

It's obvious that during the potentially long, hot summers, doors will be opened more often to help keep the daytime temperature at a healthy level and to provide airflow through the tunnel. Airflow is just as important in winter, so once or twice a week, try to open the doors to allow a natural breeze to flow through. Not only does this help prevent air

becoming stagnant, but it is also critical to reducing the threat of fungal disease building up on your winter salad leaves.

Watering

In a structure which is impervious to rain, plants will require access to this vital liquid of life. However, that this doesn't mean the process of watering need be laborious or overly time consuming, even during a heatwave (as explained below). Instead, it's about setting up systems to minimise the time and effort involved in keeping your produce sufficiently quenched all year round.

Sprinkler systems Often frowned upon as it can encourage blight on tomato plants (with moisture landing on the leaves), this system works really well for much of the year when employed in the morning, with all doors and windows opened wide. If using this method of watering, a mixed planting system (as outlined on page 118) is also preferable as it ensures a greater biodiversity from the ground up, affording greater resilience against fungal build up in the process. A sprinkler can be run either from a mains water supply or, with the aid of water pump, can circulate rainwater from your store in and around your polytunnel beds.

On the ground drip watering To enable a slow flow of water direct to roots of your plants, you can use a piped-water system. It might be a simple old hosepipe with some

Encouraging ladybirds helps to control aphids

Blackflies can be problematic in a tunnel

holes in it connected to your water butt, or it could be a sophisticated timer-controlled mains system with a manifold feeding several flat pipes with drip notches, or anything in between.

Handheld sprinkler or watering can At the more time-consuming end of the watering spectrum, this can still work well in smaller tunnels as a viable watering option. A hose pipe with a sprinkler attachment is much less effort than a watering-can however, unless

you like spending your days going back and forth to collect water. Again, if you're keen to use recycled water then a 'cheap and cheerful' pump will enable you to distribute your water-butt supply with ease.

Avoiding the build up of pests

It is a relatively common assumption that, inside a polytunnel, you are much more likely to experience a build-up of pests such as aphids. However, this is simply not the case if you employ a more biodiverse planting system with much more mix and match than block planting, if you encourage wildlife in, clean your tunnel and allow sufficient airflow. There is more on this in chapter 6 on wildlife, but wildlife, such as birds, ladybirds, ground beetles, amphibians etc., all have a vital role to play. In a biodiverse tunnel, it's much harder for one form of pest to get out of control as the problem pest is always food for something else, and therefore simply becomes a food source, rather than an out of control problem to the detriment of your plants and produce.

Dealing with extreme heat

Yes, a polytunnel will get very hot indeed in the midst of summer, especially if the doors and ventilation panels are all shut. It really doesn't take long for the sun to raise the temperature inside to an unbearable degree, so this is why planning ahead to prevent such heat build-up is key.

During the warmer months of the year, it pays to keep everything you can open to the elements, to encourage a cooling airflow as much as possible. Erring on the side of caution, in favour of a cooler tunnel overall, saves you worrying about your plants wilting when (for example) a cooler summer morning turns into an absolute scorcher when you are at work and unable to do anything about your plants. If you're worried about rabbits or other wildlife with plant-nibbling tendencies getting in overnight, then simple barriers can easily be constructed or used to provide protection.

There is a wealth of advice on dealing with extremes of heat in Chapter 2, much of which applies to protecting plants, both inside and out. Suffice to say, the techniques outlined were tested to the limit (successfully, we are pleased to add) during the heatwave of 2018, when Kim's private water supply ran almost dry. This meant that, with plentiful waterbutt reserves but a distant memory, polytunnel planting had to deal with being given a deep-soak watering just once a week. The ground cover, mulching and mixed planting enabled most of her plants inside to thrive suprisingly well despite the more challenging conditions, which just goes to show how much lower maintenance summer watering can in fact be with the right soil protection in place.

Another option for the polytunnel is the addition of mesh or vents on the sides or in the roof to provide greater airflow and cooling during periods of extreme heat.

Handling strong winds

A well-installed polytunnel will be able to stand firm against severe winds, as long as doors and all openings are kept securely shut. If you know extreme winds are forecast, it's also important to err on the side of caution and remove any potential flying debris from the vicinity, such as lightweight garden furniture or buckets, to avoid any 'collateral' damage.

Greenhouses

These valuable glass structures are also incredibly useful to have in the climate change garden. Whilst many of the same advice regarding polytunnels also applies, these structures can actually get even hotter when located in a south-facing position so that is something to bear in mind.

In my experience, aphid build-up can be more of an issue in greenhouses and so, as much as possible, you want to try and encourage beneficial wildlife such as ladybirds into your under-glass haven.

Planting in the ground is also preferable, where possible, to planting in containers, as these are often small or shallow. As a result, they can dry out rather quickly, which is far from ideal in such a torrid environment.

Seed saving

Whilst saving all of your own seed from the veg patch each year would be an extremely time-consuming and, frankly, laborious thing to do, working with at least a few crops in this way is viable. It is also extremely beneficial in the battle against the metrological volatility of the future, because the seed that you save (when done correctly) will have been genetically adapted to the growing conditions of your own individual locality. This is especially the case when done so time and time again over a period of years, with the

Saving seed from the broad bean is easy

best specimen plants grown on to flower and set seed for storage.

Seed saving used to be a firm part of the gardening calendar. It's only in more recent years that we've become so accustomed to buying seed every year. Whilst flicking through seed catalogues in the murky depths of winter (or indeed any time of the year) is undoubtedly an exciting and wholesome pastime, saving a little seed is also an increasingly important part of the climate change gardener's remit.

Seed saving is incredibly easy to do and you can save seed from more types of fruit and vegetables than you might otherwise think. The climate change credentials of saving some of your own seed are very strong indeed. No matter where you live and what you like to grow, there will be some crops that are easy to work with, producing precious seed adapted to your individual grow-your-own space.

From the beginner to the more ambitious enthusiast, here's how to get started with saving your own seed.

If you have never saved seed before, have a look at the table below that lists some of the easiest crops from which to get started.

More advanced seed saving

Once you understand the basics and get some practice under your belt, the potential to save from a much wider variety of crops is opened up before you. It's possible to save from most of the vegetables that you grow on your veg patch, though sweetcorn is a particular exception, as it requires a much wider genetic

The easiest crops from which to save seed

Crop	How to save seed
Peas and French beans	With these self-pollinating plants, simply leave a few pods in place to fatten, yellow and dry before collecting. Or, harvest the plump peas at the end of the season and leave the pods near a radiator or in an airing cupboard to dry out before storing away till the following year.
Lettuce and rocket	Another very easy seed to save. You just need to ensure that your lettuce has a long enough season to flower and set seed for you to harvest and collect. The only tricky part can be in a wetter summer, when seeds don't have the opportunity to dry in situ and go mouldy. In such weather, you'd be better off working with plants which are inside.
Tomatoes	Just harvest your tomato of choice and scoop out the seeds. You can then either leave them to dry on a piece of paper for planting in its entirety the following season or, for a slightly fiddlier method, drop the seeds into a small jar of water. The jelly-like shell rots away, leaving just the seed which can then be left out to dry.
Chillies	If you are growing a few varieties of chillis, they can cross pollinate, and the resulting offspring plants may not grow to what is called 'true to type'. This isn't a bad thing necessarily, as you will have just created your own home-grown variety, which could be milder or hotter than the parent plants.

General seed saving tips for success

Avoid FI varieties You will need to save seed from what is called open-pollinated varieties. It's easy to do — just look for seed packets which say F1 on the cover, and don't save from these plants. The reason you can't use these plants is that they have been created from a cross between two carefully selected parent plants and the resulting seed could end up with the characteristics of either and won't grow what's called 'true to type'. You just won't know what you'll end up with. Also, these seeds are protected by breeders rights so you may not propagate them or save seed. Instead, you want to save from varieties that can adapt to your own growing space and that display the genetic resilience, taste and produce qualities that you are looking for.

Pick the best-looking specimens from which to work If you think about the fact that you are going to be growing on from the offspring of the parent plants from which you chose to save seed, then it makes sense to select the healthiest, best examples of that variety of crop.

Avoid bolting plants In the same way that you want to choose the healthiest specimens, you don't want to carry on less attractive plant traits. You'll need to avoid saving from any rocket, radish and such-like that bolt early. Wait and work with the specimens that don't have such a strong element of this unattractive habit.

Nurture resilience Whilst it's obvious that you wouldn't wish to save from plants which have been weakened by disease or pests, try to pick out the plants that have shown hardy qualities in the face of adversity. So, if some of your pea plants have thrived better than others during the course of a heatwave, save from them. These are exactly the genetic qualities you want to be saving and nurturing to help your plants ride out the more extreme weather ahead. Seed saving is such an important pastime for many reasons, but this is perhaps the most important element when it comes to climate change gardening. Backyard seed savers can be the guardians of a more resilient home-grown future.

source base (that is, it requires many plants to be successful). This makes it unrealistic to save sweetcorn seed at home, because a) you wouldn't have room for hundreds of plants, and b) what on earth would you do with all that seed, even if you did.

Fortunately, seed from the brassica family, carrots, parsnips, leeks and other species can be saved reliably on your patch as they are what is known as outbreeders. This means they require a minimum of 20 plants from which to produce seed reliably. However, outbreeders have the potential to cross with other species from the same family, as they are insect-pollinated. For example, if you have purple-sprouting broccoli flowering at the same time as kale and a bee has landed on both in quick succession, then it's likely that pollen has been transferred between the two and you risk ending up with a cross. The resulting seed might prove to be okay, but it's

More advanced seed saving

Crop	Method
Beetroot, spinach Swiss chard	Biennial crops. Either leave 20 plants in the ground over winter or in the case of beetroot, harvest the roots in autumn and keep in storage. Keep back the 20 best specimens and plant out late winter/early spring for growing on. These crops are cross pollinated so do not attempt to save seed from another member of the same family (Swiss chard, leaf beet or spinach).
Carrot	Biennial crop that flowers in its second year. This plant produces the most delightfully ornamental flowers. Leave 20 plants to flower, making sure you only work with roots which have better characteristics, as (for example) a pale yellow carrot (when it should be a vibrant orange) will add those traits into the genetic mix of the seed unless you wheedle it out first. Carrot can cross with wild carrot relatives, including St Anne's lace, so for this reason, it's better to grow on your saved carrots under cover.
Kale	Most brassicas are biennials which means they will flower and set seed in their second year so they need to remain in situ during this time. The key is to ensure that when they do flower, there isn't anything else also flowering from the brassica family at the same time. Broccoli is normally the troublemaker is this regard, so it's the main plant to watch out for and cut back if it does attempt to flower at the same time. A lot of seed will be produced from 20 plants, which keeps reliably for a number of years, so your time and space investment will be paid tenfold in return.
Leek	As with carrots, this crop can be grown (and left) until the following spring in a relatively small space of ground.

Calendula will readily self-seed

Allow a few rocket plants to flower and set seed

a risk and you could end up growing a crop that turns out to be terrible in terms of taste and texture, so is best avoided.

To ensure genetic strength and vitality, and to create seed that can be grown on and bred from, a minimum of at least 20 plants is required to ensure quality and genetic variation. In reality, the likes of the Heritage Seed Library will use more like around a hundred plants, but for the home-based enthusiast, it's possible to get away with a smaller number.

The table on the left lists our suggested species for more advanced seed saving.

The best self-seeding plants

Alongside the process of collecting and storing seed over winter to be sown in the spring, there are plants that are quite capable (and possibly better off) doing it naturally for themselves. These self seeders include coriander, parsley, nasturtium, calendula etc.

Sometimes you don't need to do anything at all. Just wait for lots of lovely resilient seedlings to burst into life in spring as the weather starts to warm. All you will need to do is to gently lift and plant them on elsewhere around your veg patch.

CHAPTER
EIGHT

IN THE ORCHARD

We love our fruit trees, and for many of us, a garden is not complete without a fruit tree or two. Yet, perhaps surprisingly, our precious trees and their fruits are under increased threat from a changing climate, loss of pollinators and a rapidly multiplying number of pests and diseases.

Apples and many other top fruits are grown in temperate zones around the world, including South Africa and Australia, so being warmer in summer is not necessarily a bad thing. The problem facing them is more to do with mild winters and wet springs and a generally more erratic climate overall. For example, mention 2012 to UK apple growers and they probably shudder. That year saw one of the wettest UK summers on record. March was particularly warm and blossom appeared early but, just as the orchards were looking at their best, it started to rain and it didn't stop for six weeks. The period from April to June was the wettest ever recorded in the UK with heavy rain, gales and storms. Blossom was battered and bees didn't fly, so any surviving blossom wasn't pollinated. The average harvest was half of what it is normally and, in some areas, the crop was wiped out completely.

Left: Apple blossom in abundance

What will happen in the future as our climate becomes ever more volatile?

When you consider that the fruit trees that we choose to plant now will be reaching their best in 10 years time, and will continue to produce for many years afterwards, what should we be planting? Will our favourite heritage varieties, which were first developed 100 years ago or more, cope in a changing climate? Is it better to stick to local varieties and hope they are best placed to adapt? Should we look to new varieties, say those grown in southern France? Or should we think about rootstocks? Amidst all of these questions there are three key issues to consider: the chill factor, rootstock, and pollination.

The chill factor

Mild winters are not good news for our fruit trees. Apple and other fruits need to experience a minimum number of chill hours (a period when the temperatures range between freezing and 7°C) as this is the perfect temperature for flower bud formation. Too few hours and flower buds may open late or not at all. Each variety has its own minimum hours of chill, hence it's generally recommended that you should grow local varieties that are adapted to the climate. For example, there is no point growing northern varieties if you live in the south as the chill hours may not be achieved in a mild year. However, you can do the opposite, grow a low-chill-hour apple variety further north.

Sally has a small orchard in her walled garden

In general, apples need 1,000 chill hours. Yet, as winters get milder, there will be fewer chill hours so, looking forward, it may be wise to select varieties that need less. Some of the varieties recommended for southern Europe will grow in the UK so, when choosing new trees, think about these: Braeburn, Bramley 20, Bramley Seedling, Lord Lambourne, Saturn and Spartan. Already some of the

commercial orchards in Kent are looking to plant more of the international varieties, such as Granny Smith, Golden Delicious, Gala and Fuji. Other top-fruit species have chill requirements too. Plums are likely to be particularly hard hit as they have the longest chill requirements, while some peaches need just 50 hours.

Rootstocks

Most fruit trees are grafted. That means that a shoot has been joined to the root to create a new plant. The rootstock determines the vigour of the tree, its ultimate size, fruit-producing ability and often disease resistance, while the shoot determines the variety of fruit. There is a wide range of rootstocks for each of the fruit species.

For apples, rootstocks range from a traditional full standard (M25), which grows to 5m (16') or more, to dwarf rootstocks (M27) of just 1.5m (5') in height. MM106 is one of the most widely grown rootstocks, producing a tree up to 4m (13') in height and spread, ideal for small orchards and training into espaliers etc. Very similar, and maybe more useful in the future, is MM111, which produces a slightly taller tree. It is more vigorous and can cope with light and heavy soils, drought and wet conditions. M116 is a new rootstock that is similar to MM106 and is thought to be tolerant of a range of conditions. M26 is an all-round rootstock, producing a tree slightly smaller than MM106 but it's not great for damp

Problems in the mountains

In China, 100% hand pollination of fruit trees is common in remote mountain areas. Teams of people with paintbrushes work long hours to transfer pollen between flowers to ensure a crop of fruit. In fact, hand pollination is common across the Hindu Kush of Nepal, Pakistan and India too, where poor fruit set is experienced. The reason for this is the loss of habitats for pollinators. Hope is on the horizon, however, as farmers in the region are planting more native flowers to supply nectar to pollinators and bees are being encouraged where once they weren't.

Pollination isn't the only problem though. The Himalayas are warming up quickly and winters are milder, so fruit trees are experiencing too few chill hours and their buds don't open. Growers are having to plant orchards higher in the mountains where it's colder. Apple orchards are now found at 3,000m and above and they are running out of slopes. There are problems in Germany too, where it's traditional to plant fruit trees on alpine slopes to create shade for livestock and to have a crop. Yet with increasingly limited chill hours, farmers are now looking to grow traditional trees grafted on vigorous rootstock that produce huge crowns and deep roots, so they are more resilient. The trees may take 10 years to fruit but are more likely to survive.

ground as it is susceptible to collar rot. The dwarf rooting stock (M27) produces smaller roots, which are more susceptible to drought and are known to have shorter life, but they are good for really small spaces and large pots.

When we are thinking about climate change, we need to consider deep roots that can reach down and find water in a dry summer, so it may be better to opt for a larger tree than a dwarf one. Most UK fruit tree suppliers stick to a small range of tried-and-tested rootstocks, but if you look further afield, there is a greater choice available, some based on US, Russian and East European rootstocks, many of which may be more suited to future conditions.

Pollination woes

Research in the UK shows that apple trees are flowering an average of 17 days earlier in spring compared with 60 years ago. This risks an early-flowering variety being hit by frost or there not being enough pollinators around when the blossom opens, which is a real worry for fruit growers. An early spring may also mean insufficient chill hours. However, there is another consideration – pollination groups.

Fruit trees are grouped according to their flowering period; group 1 (or group A) being very early in April while group 7 (group G) is very late in May and early June. Each group is in blossom for about two weeks, overlapping briefly with the group in front and behind. For example, a group 3 variety will probably come into flower in late April and be pollinated by trees in groups 2, 3 and 4. Some varieties are self-fertile, so they do not need to be planted near another of the same pollination group for fruit, but for other varieties you have to ensure cross pollination. This is where a healthy insect population comes in. If you only have a few trees, you want plenty of visiting pollinators that fly on to other fruit trees in the area.

However, the shift in flowering time is not happening in a uniform manner. It's not as simple as group 1 varieties flowering a few weeks early followed by group 2 etc. Climate change is affecting varieties in a different way. For example, some group 4 varieties are flowering at the same time as group 1, while some group 3 trees have been unaffected by the changes and are flowering at their usual time. So, the practice of selecting varieties according to their pollination group is being turned upside down.

The problem is complicated further by a group of apples referred to a triploids. The Bramley seedling is an unusual variety because it has three sets of chromosomes in its cells, not the usual two sets. It's called a triploid. In fact, many of the most productive apples are triploids: Ashmead's Kernel, Belle de Boskoop, Blenheim Orange, Bramley Seedling, Jonagold, Ribston Pippin, Newtown Pippin, Winesap, and Zabergau Reinette. However, being triploid causes problems because the pollen is sterile and cannot be used for pollination, but the trees themselves still have to be pollinated to set fruit. The answer is to make sure there are suitable pollination partners growing nearby that are not triploid as well. Despite the pollination considerations, triploids tend to be vigorous, large croppers with disease resistance, and an ability to survive difficult conditions, so they may well suit a warmer climate.

Honey bees vs solitary bees

Honey bees are not the only pollinators. There are many more pollinating insects, such as hoverflies and bumble bees, but the most effective pollinators are the solitary bees. Research has found that 600 solitary bees may be able to pollinate an apple orchard as effectively as two hives of honey bees. Since hives have between 10,000 and 15,000 occupants that means that 600 solitary bees could potentially do the work of 30,000 honey bees.

Solitary bees include the mason bee (*Osmia sp*). These small, non-aggressive bees nest in cracks in walls and mortar and can be

A bee brick provides a home for mason bees

High temperatures can scorch leaves

attracted to your garden through the provision of overwinter sites. You can even buy bee bricks specially made for mason bees. These bees also need an area of moist earth in spring so they can collect building material.

To attract honey bees, have a few wild areas in your garden and plenty of nectar-rich flowers (see Chapter 6). Wild flowers are particularly important as they are better at attracting bees than cultivated varieties. If you have the space, you could think about putting a hive in your orchard. If you don't have have time to look after bees yourself, see if a local beekeeper wants a safe home for one of their hives.

Stress of extreme weather

If we experience rainy winters, it's likely that soils will be wet for longer, resulting in slow drainage and root death caused by waterlogging as trees stand in water. Wet weather can cause problems for young trees in the first few years of their establishment, especially from crown rot caused by *Phytophthora*. Some rootstocks and varieties are more susceptible, the MM106 rootstock being the most vulnerable. Symptoms include poor growth, yellowing leaves and underground, an orange-red rot.

Stormy weather may lead to more tree damage, wind rock and loss of crops if the storms occur in autumn, while unseasonably mild weather in January and February will lead to weak flowers and poor fruit set, with a greater risk of frost damage.

There are problems associated with hot, dry summers too. Fruit trees can survive a short

drought but a prolonged one causes root stress, defoliation, premature fruit fall and small fruits. The trees can experience heat stress if temperatures exceed 20°C for long periods of time, with sun-scorched leaves and damaged fruit. Lower rainfall over spring and summer will also reduce yield.

Our weather is going to be unpredictable, so there is a chance that we'll have the odd poor summer with grey skies and endless rain. This will mean less photosynthesis, less sugar and smaller fruits, as experienced in 2012. The resulting fruits may drop early or have poor storage qualities. So, as you see, the threats on the horizon are multifarious and very real indeed.

Arrival of pests and diseases

Earlier springs and later autumns mean a much longer growing season, not just for our fruit trees, but for their pests and diseases as well. Mild winters may lead to more pests successfully overwintering and becoming active earlier in the year, while warm summers may see an influx of threats from Europe, such as pear blossom weevil (*Anthonomus spilotus).*

There may also be more defoliating pests around, and where conditions favour some of our minor pests and diseases, we may see them become major issues. For example, fireblight caused by the bacterium *Erwinia amylovora* is present in the UK, but not at the level seen in the USA. The bacteria overwinter in bark cankers and then, in spring the bacteria ooze out and infect the tree's inner bark by way of the blossom. At the moment, its spread is restricted by cold weather around the time of flowering. But as springs become warmer and more humid, conditions will favour the bacteria, which are spread by bees and rain.

Wet winters may see a surge in scab caused by *Venturia inequalis*, although it will be limited by hot, dry summers. Powdery mildew, too, may become a problem as it likes hot, dry summers. This common disease of apples and pears turns young shoots grey-white, distorting the leaves and causing the blossom to drop. The causative agent, a fungus, overwinters in the buds and then becomes active in spring.

Spread a thick layer of mulch around the tree but not right up to the trunk as this can cause rot.

Protect your trees - how to provide resilience

Soils around fruit trees in gardens and orchards are just as important as in the veg plot, so keep them covered. Spread a thick hardwood chip mulch around the trees to a diameter of one meter in spring to retain moisture and protect the roots from extremes of temperatures. This controls the weeds too, which will compete with tree roots for water and nutrients. If you source wood chips rather than use your own, make sure the chips have not been taken from wood infected with honey fungus. There is some evidence that willow chip mulch helps to combat apple scab so that's one source to look out for.

A diverse orchard

As mentioned before, diversity is often the key to success. If you are planning a new orchard, however small, try to choose a wide range of varieties as this will make your orchard more resilient. A diverse orchard will support a wider range of insects and other animals too.

A medlar will boost diversity within an orchard

If you are choosing apples, mix up the dessert, cider and cooking varieties and their time of harvest, and choose different pollination groups to ensure successful cross pollination. Late flowering, late-maturing varieties generally need more chill hours, especially the cider varieties, so these are better suited to more northern sites. Think carefully about your choice of rootstock too. As well as mixing up the apples, include a good mix of other fruits, such as pears, plums, damsons, medlars, quinces and mulberries, and maybe some nuts.

You need to think carefully about the siting of a new orchard. Try to avoid exposed windy sites or plant the fruit trees behind a wind break. Spend time preparing the soil to make sure it drains well. A warm, sunny spot will attract more pollinators. You can even plant the odd crab apple to provide extra pollination opportunities. Varieties, such as Golden Hornet, Winter Hornet and Red Sentinel, look good in autumn as well as being functional in spring.

Other fruit options

As well as the usual apples, pears and plums, there are other fruits worth considering for your climate change garden:

Apricots Once these fruits could only be grown against south-facing walls, but there are new varieties that can be planted in the open. They need an open, sunny aspect with well-drained soil. In the right place, a five-year-old apricot tree can potentially yield 500 fruits or more. Look for North American varieties that end in -cot, such as Flavourcot and Tomcot. The risk with apricot is the early flowering. Sally's fan-trained apricot on her garden wall is often flowering in February and she has had to resort to hand pollination due to lack of insects.

Almond More people are growing almonds. They are surprisingly easy to grow, but crops can be a little hit and miss as they need a warm, dry summer. The trees like a sunny position with a well-drained soil, but are drought tolerant once established. Try a variety such as Robijn that is self-fertile, has sweet-tasting nuts, and is resistant to peach leaf curl.

Apricots may become more reliable

Asian pear or nashi (*Pyrus pyrifolia*) An easy to grow, long-lived tree reaching 5m (16') in height. The early blossom has good frost resistance. The trees start fruiting from the second year and the aromatic fruits, ready in July, are crisp and juicy. Look out for US varieties Lizzie and Beauty, and Japanese varieties Hosui, Shinko and Shinseiki.

Cherries Cherries have a lower chill requirement than apples. Those varieties suited to Australia, California, and the Mediterranean only need 300 hours while others need 700+ chill hours. The downside is that they may be

Cherries require fewer chill hours than apples

The crisp and juicy Asian pear

susceptible to cold, wet winters and frost, as the blossom is early.

Figs This fruit needs a warm, south-facing wall as heat is needed for the fruit to ripen. It is recommended that the roots are restricted to limit the growth of the tree and stimulate the formation of fruit. This happens naturally at the base of a wall, but you could achieve the same by planting it in an open-bottomed box or in a pit in the ground bounded by paving slabs. The plants are self-fertile. There are a number of hardy varieties, including the widely grown Brown Turkey, Brunswick and Violetta.

Kiwi fruits These vigorous climbing plants need space and a sunny aspect. Some varieties, such as Jenny, are self-fertile, but others have just male or female flowers. The young shoots are at risk of frost damage and need protection. Fruits appear three to four years after planting. They do not ripen on the plant so need to be picked and left to ripen indoors.

Pears Pears have frost-hardy blossom, but they are grafted onto quince rootstocks that need moisture, especially in spring. In a dry spring, it's recommended that pears are watered from the time the flower buds appear for six weeks to improve the yield. In a dry

Fruit trees in containers

If you have a small garden and no space for an apple tree, then what about a fruit tree in a container? It needs to be grafted on dwarfing rootstock, such as M9 and M26, rather than the ultra dwarfing M27 which may not thrive in a hot summer. Dwarf trees may not live as long as some of the more vigorous rootstocks but they start producing fruit more quickly. You can also grow cherry, pear, plum, damson, peach, nectarine, and apricot on dwarf rootstocks as well as figs and lemons.

Ideally, the pot needs to be at least 50cm (20") in diameter. A clay pot may be better as it retains water. Tip some drainage materials into the bottom and backfill with a good compost mixed with grit and mulch with gravel or fleece. Feed every two weeks with a liquid tomato or sea-weed feed and place in full sun in a sheltered position. In autumn, the less hardy apricot, peach and lemon can be moved under cover or protected. It's important not to let the roots become pot bound, so move to a larger pot every other year or prune back the roots. The key to successful pot fruit is careful watering – not too much, but don't allow the compost to dry out.

summer, they should be given one bucket per tree daily. Quince C rootstock produces a smaller tree which fruits more quickly.

Peaches These fruits have been grown in the UK for hundreds of years. They need a warm, sheltered spot, ideally trained against a south-facing wall but in mild areas you may get away with growing them as a bush. Like apricots, they need a short chill period for flowering. Flowers appear early and are at risk of frost so they need to be protected with fleece. The trees also need protection from spring rain, which can bring on leaf curl.

Gages Plums and damsons need the most chill hours so they are most affected by mild winters. The close relative, the gage, may be a good alternative. As well as being incredibly tasty, they are suited to drier climates. French varieties of gage include Outlins Gage (yellow) and the self-fertile Reine Claude de Bavay.

Pomegranate This plant is surprisingly hardy, with varieties, such as Provence, being hardy to -15°C. The self-fertile plants should be given a sunny, sheltered spot. One of the difficulties with this fruit is that it needs heat for the fruit to ripen, so long hot and dry summers followed by warm autumn temperatures of 13–16°C are needed for harvesting in October and November.

Growing olives

Think Mediterranean gardens and olive trees spring to mind, so can we grow them more

Damsons have a high chill requirement

widely in a warmer UK? Olives are found growing high in slopes in southern Europe and can withstand a cold winter. In fact, like many other tree and shrub species, they actually need a chill period (under 10°C/50°F) of at least three months, with fluctuations between day and night temperatures, in order to flower and fruit, which is why container-grown olives kept in conservatories are unlikely to flower. Equally, prolonged cold can also inhibit fruiting. Those grown outside will flower easily, but a good summer is needed to get the fruits to ripen.

Olives grow best in poor sandy-type soils in a sheltered, sunny location. They will grow in clay soils but you need to avoid areas that get waterlogged in winter as they don't like it cold

Olives for eating or oil?

You can grow olives for eating and pressing. Remember that ripe olives when eaten raw will taste quite different to commercial olives, as they are picked, steeped in water to remove the bitter taste or cured in salty water. It's very easy to make oil. Simply gather the ripe fruit, crush and squeeze through a press. Newly pressed oil is very green initially but this fades to golden yellow. You will need about 5kg (11lb) of fruits to make a litre (1.8 pints) of oil.

English olive oil

Kent is already home to many vineyards and now the olive grove invasion is under way. South East England has the driest climate in the UK and some farmers are planting for the future as it will take many years for olive trees to reach peak fruiting. For example, more than 200 olive trees have been planted in the Isle of Oxney near Tenterton, Kent with the hope of producing the UK's first extra virgin olive oil in the near future.

and wet. One way around this can be to half plant the root ball and build up around the plant with more free-draining soil.

Most garden olives are grown in pots, in which they do well, because of their small root systems and drought-hardy nature. Give them a large pot with lots of drainage holes, filled with loam-based compost and grit, or alternatively, create a bottomless box around the root ball with sleepers or paving slabs.

Olives should be watered and fed between February and May to encourage fruiting and should not be allowed to dry out in summer as the fruits will shrivel and drop. Trees start producing fruits when they are three to five years old, fruiting on the tips of the previous year's growth, so any pruning

will reduce fruiting. The crop should be thinned to three-quarters of the fruits per 30cm (12") length of branch within three weeks of flowering to ensure a crop that ripens and doesn't drop.

Keeping a potted olive watered in winter is also important, so don't let it dry out. Growers have found that olives can survive extremely low temperatures for several weeks so long as they are watered. Prolonged cold weather will cause the leaves to drop and the bark to split and there may be dieback in young plants. However, cold-damaged plants should regrow from dormant buds, but won't flower and fruit as well in the following months.

Which olive to grow?

There are more than 800 cultivars, and as you

Olives grown in large pots

would expect, there are some that are more cold hardy or tolerant of wet soil than others. Most can tolerate -1°C (30°F) and some are hardier still. If in doubt grow in containers so they can be moved into a protected space when needed.

Arbequina A small, self-fertile Spanish tree of medium vigour, cold hardy and adaptable. It's able to cope with poor soil and is a good pollinator. The small fruits appear from four years, and are good for olive oil.

Cipressino From Puglia, Italy with a vigorous upright habit. It's very hardy and copes well with coastal conditions. Its black olives make a fine olive oil.

Frantoio A small-to-medium tree with large fruit from Tuscany, Italy. It's thought to be adaptable to UK weather.

Picual (also known as Blanco, Nevadillo, Picua) This Spanish olive adapts to diverse environments and responds well to regenerative pruning if damaged by snow fall. It has a good resistance to cold, bacteria and damp soils. It is self-fertile, but also pollinated by Leccino. High yielding and good for a fruity, aromatic oil.

Leccino This popular open, semi-pendulous variety from Tuscany is easy to grow and tolerant of a wide range of conditions. It's self-sterile so needs a pollinator and produces

Olives may become a common sight in gardens

high quality olives for eating and oil.

Maurino Another Tuscan variety that will cross pollinate Leccino. The oil is delicate and soft.

Pendolino This Tuscan olive has a compact weeping habit, so ideal for small places. It's self-sterile and needs a pollinator. It produces black olives for eating and oil.

Grapevines

As the climate warms up, the ability to grow grapevines in new areas increases. Already vines are grown across England and Wales and more areas are planned in the coming years. So, are grapes a good option and could you plant a micro-vineyard?

Many people already grow grapevines in glasshouses and conservatories, but for planting outside you need to have the right spot. That's somewhere warm, sunny, sheltered, ideally against a south-facing wall with well-drained soil or growing up a pergola or gazebo in a sheltered, sunny spot. Like many Mediterranean plants, grapevines can tolerate the cold, but need a free-draining soil.

It's perfectly possible to establish a small vineyard in a garden or allotment

Once they are established, the vines don't need watering and they can cope with infertile soils as their deep roots will penetrate into the subsoil, bringing up nutrients so they don't need feeding. In fact, too much nitrogen results in more leaf and less fruit. There are two types of grapevine, one that produces dessert grapes and the other for wine. Some dessert varieties to consider include Boskoop Glory, Muscat Hamburg, Strawberry Grape, and Vitis 'Brant' AGM. There are also some dual-purpose grape varieties, such as Phoenix, Regent and Theresa, that are sweet when grown in a conservatory or greenhouse but outside they are better for wine.

On a visit to the National Trust's Knightshays garden in Devon, Sally noticed a micro vineyard amongst the vegetables. Micro vineyards are popping up in gardens and allotments across southern England and there's likely to be even more in the future. You can plant as many as 30 vines in a 50 square metre (538 square feet) plot. Given a well established vine can produce 1.5–2 kg (3lb 3oz–4lb 4 oz) of grapes, enough fruit for 2 to 3 bottles, you could make upwards of 60+ bottles of wine a year from your tiny plot.

CHAPTER
NINE

TREES FOR THE FUTURE

Walk along a Spanish street in the height of summer and you will be very grateful for the cooling shade cast by trees. Trees are an important feature of Mediterranean towns and cities. It's long been known that they can help to reduce the temperature by shading the ground from direct sunlight and cooling the air through the evaporation of water from their leaves (transpiration). They are so effective that the difference in temperature under trees compared with a nearby unshaded area on a hot summer day can be as much as 14°C (25.2°F). There are further benefits. Trees can be planted so that they shade buildings and reduce the demand for air conditioning in summer. Cities are already several degrees warmer than the surrounding areas and they are going to experience even higher temperatures as a result of climate change. By increasing the green canopy of trees, the so-called urban forest, cities could help to offset some of these changes.

Looking ahead, trees are going to be an important feature of the climate change garden also, especially those gardens with a southerly aspect, helping to provide essential shade

A river of green runs through Barcelona, Spain but more trees will be needed in the years to come

in summer, valuable shelter from wind, as well as slowing water and reducing storm water run-off. Organisations such as the Forestry Commission, Woodland Trust and the Royal Horticultural Society in the UK and the United States Forest Service are looking ahead to how trees will fair in the future and some of their research can help our own decisions over which trees we should be choosing to plant in our gardens.

Changing conditions

Trees are long-lived features of gardens, parks and the wider landscape. An oak tree planted today could still be around in several hundred years time. The conditions that the adult tree experiences are going to be very different to those of today. It's expected that trees will grow faster because of the longer growing seasons, the added warmth, plus the higher

Oaks under threat

A 300-year old veteran oak was a mere acorn during the latter part of the Little Ice Age and will have experienced many storms, droughts and floods during its long, majestic life. Now it faces a new threat with a period of rapid environmental change and new pests and diseases that could easily threaten its continued survival via climate change.

It was the arrival of a new disease, Dutch elm disease in the 1970s that virtually wiped out the elm across Europe, changing the landscape of the countryside. The disease, spread by elm bark beetles, has wiped out millions of elms across North America too. More recently, ash dieback (Chalara disease) has emerged as a major threat.

Since the 1980s the health of oak trees has been declining and now the threat comes from a disease called Acute Oak Decline, which was first reported in East Anglia, but has since been seen across central and southern England. The causes are unclear as it seems to be a multifaceted problem, but experts agree that the general health of the tree is important for overall resilience against such threats, as soil and soil life, root health, waterlogging, drought and the presence of pollutants in the air and water can all weaken the tree and affect its ability to withstand disease. Both the pedunculate oak (*Quercus robur*) and sessile oak (*Q. petraea*) are affected, the symptoms

being vertical weeping fissures that seep a black fluid down the trunk, a so-called stem bleed. Usually found close by are the larval galleries of the buprestid beetle (*Agrilus biguttatus*). The affected trees tend to be 50 years or older and have been weakened by other factors. Research shows the infected trees to be growing mostly in the drier parts of country that have longer and warmer growing seasons, on ground that is seasonally waterlogged or has high clay content. There is also a link to a higher levels of atmospheric pollutants, such as nitrous oxides and sulphur.

Magnolia blossom appears in early spring and is often damaged by frost

levels of carbon dioxide that will boost photosynthesis. But long summer droughts could restrict summer growth and cause cracks in timber, making the loss of branches more likely. Buildings near trees may be at greater risk of subsidence as trees extract more water in a dry year. Buds may open early, but this puts susceptible trees at greater risk of frost damage, especially those growing on south-facing slopes.

With an increase in frequency of storms and strong winds, it is likely that more trees will be damaged or even uprooted, especially if winters are wetter and soil waterlogged.

The impact of climate change will be seen in declining tree health, difficulty in getting trees to establish and the death of mature trees as a result of environmental stress. A warmer spring and autumn mean that insect pests may be able to have more broods of young per year and this will lead to more damage to trees in the form of defoliation and so forth. Insect pests that appear in summer from mainland Europe may be able to survive overwinter and become active early the following year.

The wet winters will bring more disease, especially fungal diseases, which could take advantage of trees that are weakened by drought and quicken their death. Most at risk are tree species that are least tolerant of drought and those growing in shallow, well drained soils in the southern half of England. Trees growing in the other regions should be more resilient and gardeners based in the Midlands and northern regions will find their trees are more productive and they will be able to tap into the opportunity to grow a wider range of species.

What should we be planting?

Looking ahead, it's expected that the South East and East of England will enjoy warmer, drier summers, rather like those currently experienced in southern France, which will cause problems for trees. Elsewhere in England and Wales, the climate will be more like that of North West France.

On a commercial scale, foresters are already looking at the species they are planting now, so that they will be able to cope with the changing conditions. In the south, there may be more ash, beech, Corsican pine, wild cherry, oaks, Norway maple, sweet chestnut and Scot's pine, but by 2080 under the worst-case scenario, even the most resilient of species, such as beech, sessile oak and Scot's pine may fail. Further north, the forests will see more alder, ash, beech, wild cherry, Corsican pine, Douglas fir, lodgepole pine and Scot's pine. However, some common species, such as downy birch and sycamore, may not fare so well, while Japanese larch and red cedar are expected to be unsuitable for use in England by 2080.

It will become increasingly important to source seed or saplings carefully. Normally, the advice is to choose local sources as the trees will be better adapted to the conditions, but as the climate changes, it will be better to source from an area that has a climate similar to the predicted climate of the future. Despite the risk from importing pest and diseases, many foresters are recommending that material is sourced from two degrees latitude south of the site where they will be planted. For example, if you live in northern England or Scotland, source from southern England, if you live in the south, source from France. Do also be aware of the risk of frost that comes with the extended growing seasons, as buds may burst earlier leaving the young leaves vulnerable to a late frost. Try to choose species that are less sensitive to frost and

The early spring blossom of acacia in the south of England

work on mainly south or east-facing slopes.

The role of the arboretum

The role of arboreta in the UK is becoming increasingly important as we try to predict which species will grow well in the future. Many different species from around the world are grown in arboreta and their experts are well placed to judge which could be grown more widely and successfully in the UK moving forwards.

Some of the species that may thrive in 30 to 50 years include:

- Golden mimosa (*Acacia baileyan*) from New South Wales, Australia
- Red alder (*Alnus rubra*) from western North America

- Paper birch (*Betula papyrifera*) from North America
- Shagbark hickory (*Carya ovata*) from the eastern United States
- Turkish hazel (*Corylus colurna*) from South East Europe
- Italian cypress (*Cupressus sempervirens*) from the eastern Mediterranean
- Cider gum (*Eucalyptus gunnii*) from Tasmania
- Oriental beech (*Fagus orientalis*) from eastern Europe and western Asia
- Green ash (*Fraximus pennsylvanica*) and white ash (*Fraxinus americana*) from North America and narrow-leaved ash (*Fraxinus augustifolia*) from central and southern Europe
- Black walnut (*Juglans nigra*) from eastern North America
- Patagonian oak or noble beech (*Nothfagus obliqua*) from South America
- Hop hornbeam (*Ostrya carpinifolia*) from southern Europe
- Paulownia (*Paulownia tomentosa*) from China
- Serbian spruce (*Picea omorika*) from the Balkans
- Wild pear (*Pyrus pyraster*) from Europe
- Tulip tree (*Liriodendron tulipifera*) from eastern North America

Botanists often notice that some species that are restricted to certain soils or habitats may

Italian cypress may thrive in a warmer UK

grow well in an arboretum in a completely different part of the world. Often a species' restricted distribution is due to other factors. For example, the fact that they can survive in an alkaline soil puts them at a competitive advantage over other species. They could grow in other soils or even other habitats, but they are not able to outcompete other species. Sometimes there are surprises, for example a specimen may survive a drought or an extremely hard winter against the odds, so that is the tree from which to save seed or take cuttings.

Planting new trees

Choosing the best time to plant your tree is your first decision. Bare-rooted trees are only sold in autumn and winter and have to be planted immediately or heeled into the ground until conditions are right. Container grown trees can be planted all year, but they will need a lot of care if planted in late spring and summer. Ideally you want to plant your new tree when the soil is moist, but not waterlogged, and you definitely don't want to plant while the ground is frozen. Although, if plant too early in the winter, you risk your tree sitting in cold, waterlogged ground for the rest of the winter.

In recent years, Sally has struggled to find the right slot to plant her new fruit trees on her heavy soils. Torrential rain in November and December has left her soil waterlogged for much of winter, so she has ended up planting in late February, which didn't give the trees long to get established before the weather started to warm up.

Drought is always a concern after planting a new tree and it's increasingly likely that your new trees will have to cope with a hot summer, so a good start means they can establish a large root system as soon as possible. You will also have to make sure that drought or waterlogging doesn't restrict early growth.

As mentioned many times already, you need to make sure that the soil is well drained and has plenty of organic matter. The soil should be watered before you plant as you don't want the plants struggling to take up water. It's also beneficial to soak bare-rooted trees for 30 minutes before planting and to water a container-grown plant. The hole you dig needs to be no wider than twice the diameter of the root ball, but no deeper than the rootball itself. Make the hole square too, as that helps the roots to grow into the surrounding soil. Also, it is important to make sure the soil around the hole is not compacted, if it is, the water will sit around the roots and not drain away, so fork the soil around the hole, but don't disturb it.

Position your stake (see below) and place the tree in the hole. If it's a container plant, scrap away loose soil on the top and tease out the roots. Make sure the tree is at the correct level in the ground, never deeper than the original level, so look for the mark on the stem indicating where it started to grow above ground. Sprinkle the roots with mycorrhizal powder and sugar (see below) and backfill the hole with soil, gently treading the ground to get rid of any air holes and pockets where water could collect. At this point, you don't want any organic matter in the hole as it has a tendency to shrink and allow water to collect inside. Instead, spread a layer of mulch around, but not up to the plant to keep in moisture and suppress weeds. You may also need to fix rabbit or deer-protection spirals.

If you are concerned that the site may be liable to waterlogging or even flood, plant the tree on a mound so that water runs safely away. Pile up the soil to create a mound that about 30cm (1') above the surface of the soil and with a diameter of 1m (3'3"). If you are planting a container-grown tree, plant half the root ball above ground and mound up the soil to cover it.

Mycorrhizal root treatment

Lots has been written about the benefits of applying a mycorrhizal fungal powder to roots before planting. Some gardeners swear by it and apply it to the roots of all their transplants and even use it on seeds, while others consider it a waste of time. The USDA Forest Service in the US has found inoculating seedlings prior to planting has increased early growth.

The theory behind the treatment is sound: you want your tree roots to associate with mycorrhizal fungi as soon as possible. The fungi are fast growing and will soon produce a network of hyphae through the soil to take up water and nutrients and give the tree a good start. It's thought to be particularly important for bare-rooted stock as some of their roots will have been damaged as they were levered out of the ground. Typically,

Learning from the past

Ultimately, to hedge our bets against the uncertainties of the future, it's best to plant lots of different kinds of trees as we cannot be certain which species will thrive and which will not. Experts point to problems in the past where people have planted too many of the same kind of tree. For example, urban landscapers often plant whole streets with just one species of tree. If a disease hits, all the trees in the street could die, so the lesson to learn is to plant a mixture of species. They can still be native species, but must be diverse

these trees suffer from transplant shock as the plant is unable to take up water and nutrients from the soil until its roots have started to grow. A treatment of mycorrhizal fungi can help container-grown trees and shrubs too. These plants can be slow to get away, often because they don't have a large enough root system to support the shoots. A large container-grown plant may be rooted in a small pot, so the roots take time to settle and start growing into the surrounding soil and this is achieved more quickly with mycorrhizal fungi.

There is no doubt that the presence of these mutualistic fungi are beneficial to most plants and the soil. The fungal hyphae extend

Sugar and biochar

Another treatment that may be effective in helping your tree to establish is a sprinkling of sugar around the roots before you backfill the hole – yes sugar! This has been found to stimulate the growth of mycorrhizal fungi and may even fuel the growth of new roots. And another option is to add biochar to the planting hole (see Chapter 4). The recommended dosage is 5–10% biochar by volume in the planting hole before you backfill. Unlike organic matter, biochar doesn't degrade so there is no loss of soil volume.

through the soil, binding the soil particles together creating a better soil structure and improved water-holding capacity, which provides better drought resilience. However, you don't have to buy commercial powders. Any soil that has had plants growing in it should have fungal spores present, as will a compost rich in woody materials. And if you don't have any compost, you could collect some leaf mould from under trees and hedgerows and use that as an inoculum for the new plant.

Commercially, there are several mycorrhizal fungal products containing a mix of UK-sourced mycorrhizal fungi, including powders that you sprinkle over roots or make up into a drench or gel. The idea behind these products is to treat the roots of new trees before they go into the ground, so the roots are pre-inoculated with the right fungi.

Staking your trees

It is always recommended to stake your new tree at the same time as planting unless it's a small sapling. A tree can take several years to establish a decent root network and to anchor itself firmly in the ground, so a stake prevents the plant from moving in the wind and damaging new roots. Once you are certain the plant is well established you can remove the stake.

There are several different approaches to staking. The most common method is to place a single stake, one third the height of the tree beside the tree with a gap of 3-4cm (1.5") between the tree stem and the stake, secured with a tie. This height allows the upper part of the tree to move in the wind and causes the stem to thicken. But if you have a tree with a long, flexible stem that could be damaged in the wind, use a taller stake and cut it back in a few years. Many people use an angled short stake, driven in at 45° into the prevailing wind. This is the recommended method on slopes and windy locations. If you have a container-grown tree or a large root-balled tree, you can use two stakes, one each side of the plant secured by long ties or a crossbar to give greater support

Aftercare

There are a few things you can do to ensure the survival of your tree. Make sure the area around the trunk is well mulched to retain moisture and keep down weeds. Check the ties are secure but not too tight and that the stake is not rubbing the tree bark. It's important to water your new plants through their first summer, regardless of the weather. Often the surface layer can be moist, but deep down the soil around the roots may be dry. Some people recommend irrigation tubes to get the water straight to the roots, but it's better to apply it to the surface of the soil with a watering can fitted with a rose to mimic rainfall. That way the water percolates slowly through the soil. Also, it's much better to give a good drenching once a week than to sprinkle a little water everyday. Do take care though, as you don't want to add too much as the young roots won't extend out that far in search of water. You can check you are using the right amount as the water should drain away within 10 minutes.

Giving your trees a helping hand

Our garden trees are going to experience a lot of stress – dry hot summers, wet winters, the occasional big freeze or a late frost. This stress weakens your trees, so they are more likely to succumb to disease or pests. You can try to boost their health by looking after microorganisms in the soil around their roots.

Newly planted tree with stake, tie and mulch

We suggested adding biochar to the planting hole of a new tree, but all adult trees could also stand to benefit. An enriched biochar mixed with fungi, seaweed and worm casts has been applied to the soil around ash trees to help them combat ash dieback and early results look promising. There is no harm and lots of potential benefit to adding biochar to the root zone of older trees to help reduce the impact of environmental stress and make them more resilient to disease. Another treatment is compost tea. Compost tea is full

the canopy, each hole around 8cm (3") wide and 25cm (10") deep, and these are backfilled with sand, gravel, organic matter, biochar or a mycorrhizal fungal inoculant.

A low carbon way of cooling your home

Trees can be effective in reducing the heat load on your home in summer. A shaded wall can be several degrees cooler than an unshaded wall and is far more effective than using curtains to shade a room. Trees can be planted on the east, south and west of a house:

- East planting will shade the house in the morning, although the temperature reduction is not so great.

- South planting means shade in the late morning to early afternoon, but trees need to be planted near the house or they have to be taller species so they cast a long enough shadow to shade your home. You need to avoid this aspect if you have solar panels on your roof or a passive solar system in the house.

- West planting is ideal as the tree casts a shadow during the afternoon when temperatures are peaking and so will have greatest effect on reducing temperatures inside the house. You can plant smaller trees or large shrubs on this side as the sun is lower in the sky and the trees cast longer shadows.

of nutrients and beneficial microorganisms and by watering around your trees, you can get nutrients and micro-organisms direct to the root zones.

Vertical mulching

This method of mulching was mentioned in Chapter 4, and it's an effective way of improving the soil around trees that are looking stressed, for example, showing poor growth, branch dieback and environmental stress. The vertical holes help to aerate the soil, improve drainage and reduce compaction around the tree, especially where soil has been subject to flooding or vehicle traffic. Earth augers are used to drill holes at regular intervals under

Natural shading from trees reduces the heat load on a house in summer

A deciduous tree with a heavy canopy is best as it casts a dense shade in summer and because they lose their leaves, the sun can still penetrate the branches in winter to warm up the house. Many landscape architects recommend growing slower-maturing species. Although they take longer to reach full height, they tend to have deeper roots and stronger branches so will be less prone to drought and wind or snow damage. A container-grown tree of around 2m (6'6") in height planted a few metres from the house will start to shade the ground floor windows in its first year.

Shady areas

Trees can cast shadows over paths, drive-ways and patios to provide welcome shade on the hottest of days. Shady areas increase the diversity of conditions in your garden and allow you to grow a wider variety of plants. Aim to create a dappled rather than dense shade so, enough light reaches the ground to enable you to have an understorey, while reducing heat stress and cooling the soil. Trees, such as silver birch, have an open canopy that lets the light penetrate. The trees will intercept some of the rain, so it will be necessary to mulch and water in summer.

Trees for the climate change garden

Species	Features	Site conditions
Mimosa (*Acacia dealbata*)	Fast growing, evergreen tree to 6m (20'). Fern-like leaves and clouds of yellow fragrant flowers in early spring.	Full sun and well-drained soil. Tolerates most soil types other than chalk. Not hardy in very cold winters, but will reshoot from the base if badly damaged.
Norway maple (*Acer platanoides*)	Naturalised. Large deciduous tree to 20⁺m (66'), good for autumn colour. Grown widely in urban areas.	Full sun, wide range of soils, tolerates limey soils and air pollution, wind and exposed sites, but not waterlogging.
Sycamore (*Acer pseudoplatanus* 'Brilliantissimum')	Small, slow growing tree, spreading to 6m (20'), salmon pink leaves in spring that become dark green by summer, with winged red fruits in autumn, good for smaller gardens,	Ideal for full sun to partial shade, moist to well drained fertile soil, tolerant of dry, partial shade.
Red maple (*Acer rubrum*)	From North America. Deciduous tree reaching 12m (40') with great autumn colour.	Hardy and adaptable tree, coping with wide range of conditions, full sun to partial shade, most soils, but not very dry soils, copes with wet and waterlogged soils.
Alder (*Alnus glutinosa*)	Large, native deciduous tree reaching 20m (66'). Nitrogen-fixing species.	Full sun to partial shade, all soils, tolerant of waterlogging and wet sites, plus windy, exposed sites.
River birch (*Betula nigra*)	From South East USA. A deciduous tree with unique, shaggy cinnamon-coloured bark, like a peeling skin, creating a fluffy appearance. Pyramidal tree reaching 7–12m (23–40').	Hardy. Full sun to partial shade on well drained to wet soil. Grows well on waterlogged or boggy ground, but also copes with arid tree pits in urban streets.
Silver birch (*Betula pendula*)	Fast growing, native deciduous tree reaching 25m (82'). Single stemmed, but can be planted close in groups for a multi-stemmed appearance, narrow conical shape.	Hardy. Good for growing in shade, but also for creating shade. Full sun to dappled shade, well-drained soil, all aspects. Copes with dry, partial shade.
Himalayan birch (*Betula utilis* 'Snow Queen')	A small garden tree that grows to 7m (23') in 20 years. Easily recognised for its snow-white bark providing all year round colour. Green leaves and yellow catkin in spring and yellow leaves in autumn. Casts a dappled shade.	Hardy. Full sun to partial shade, sheltered or exposed sites on wide range of soils.

Trees for the climate change garden

Species	Features	Site conditions
Northern catalpa (*Catalpa speciosa*)	From North America. Easy to grow. Better choice than *Catalpa bignonoides*.	Full sun to partial shade. Tolerant of a wide range of soils and soil conditions. Can cope with dry summers and flooding.
Atlas cedar (*Cedrus atlantica* 'Glauca')	Impressive tree with silvery blue foliage reaching more than 20m (66'). Suitable for large gardens and parks.	Thrives on most soils and is drought tolerant. Does not like waterlogging.
Judas tree (*Cercis siliquastrum*)	Southern Europe and Western Asia. Small tree reaching 10m (32'), masses of pink flowers in spring, attractive heart-shaped leaves and good autumn colour.	Sunny position on most soils. Copes with dry conditions but not wet soil.
Hawthorn including cockspur hawthorn (*Crataegus crus-galli*) and broad-leaved cockspur hawthorn (*Crataegus x persimilis* 'Prunifolia' AGM)	From North America. Small, wide-spreading tree, slow growing to 6-8m (20-26'), dense branches with thorns, useful for creating a shelter belt or screen. Good for flowers, colour and berries for wildlife.	Hardy. Sun or partial sun, with any well drained soil. Deep rooting tree that is drought resistant.
Snow gum (*Eucalyptus pauciflora* subsp. *niphophila*)	From Australia. Fast-growing evergreen, growing to 6–8m (20–26'), with aromatic foliage.	Needs a sunny and sheltered aspect with moist, well drained soil. Drought tolerant, but can cope with poorly drained soils too.
Spindle tree (*Euonymus europaeus*)	Native, deciduous, small tree found in hedgerows, reaches 4m (13'). Great autumn colour with amazing pink-winged fruits.	Full sun to partial shade, but best colour in sunny spots. Any well drained soil. Copes with dry partial shade.
Maidenhair tree (*Ginkgo biloba*)	From China. Large, deciduous species reaching 25m (82') in 20 to 50 years.	Needs sunny aspect. Can cope with exposed sites. Prefers well-drained soils. Drought tolerant.
Honey locust (*Gleditsia triacanthos* 'Sunburst')	Attractive, fast-growing, deciduous tree with open structure that creates dappled shade, grows to 8m (26') (other varieties taller). Great for urban gardens and as a street tree.	Sunny aspect with moist, well-drained soils of all types and pH. Pollution and drought tolerant.

Trees for the climate change garden

Species	Features	Site conditions
Japanese raisin tree (*Hovenia dulcis*)	Small tree from China and Mongolia where it's used in reforestation schemes.	Full sun on well drained soil, hardy, tolerant of sandy soils.
Holly (*Ilex aquifolium*)	Slow-growing, evergreen tree with masses of berries in autumn. Needs a male holly tree nearby to get berries for the non-self fertile varieties. Good varieties include broad-leaved silver holly 'Argentea marginata', that reaches 15m (49').	Hardy. Sun or partial shade, with moist, well drained, moderately-fertile, humus-rich soil. Tolerates dry, partial shade. Copes with wind and storms. Grows well in urban and coastal locations.
Rocky Mountain juniper (*Juniperus scopulorum*)	From North America. Upright, pencil-shaped tree, reaching 10m (33'), with blue foliage.	Very hardy. Sun or partial shade. Well-drained soils. Drought tolerant.
Pride of India or Golden rain tree (*Koelreuteria paniculata*)	From China. Medium-sized, deciduous tree reaching 10–12m (33–40'), with good autumn colour. Good for pollinators.	Hardy. Full sun, well-drained moist soils. Drought resistant and good for calcareous soils.
Sweet gum (*Liquidamber stryraciflua*)	From North America. Fast-growing deciduous tree, 10–20m (33–66'), similar in appearance to a maple and grown for autumn colour.	Sunny aspect on moist, well-drained fertile soils, especially moist, acidic loam. Likes warm summers. Hardy in UK, although may need some protection in extreme cold spells.
Tulip tree (*Liriodendron tulipifera*)	From eastern North America. Vigorous, deciduous, low-water demanding tree that reaches 12–20m (40–66'). Member of magnolia family. The saddle-shaped leaves have good autumn colour. Tulip-shaped yellow green flowers appear after 20 years.	All aspects in sun and partial shade, well-drained soils of all types, although prefers acid to neutral. No great drought resistance but likes a sunny position.
Osage orange (*Maclura pomifera*)	Slow-growing trees reaching 6m (20') in 10 years and eventually 18m (59'). Good for hedging and wind breaks.	Hardy. Sunny spots with well-drained soils.
Tupelo (*Nyssa sylvatica*)	From North America. Medium-sized deciduous tree, 10–15m (33–49'), with spectacular autumn colour.	Full sun, fertile moist soils. Copes with waterlogging.
Empress tree (*Paulownia tomentosa*)	Fast-growing, deciduous, upright tree reaching 12m (40'). Bright green leaves with pink flowers.	Sunny spots with fertile, well drained soil. Tolerant of atmospheric pollution.

Trees for the climate change garden

Species	Features	Site conditions
Hop tree (*Ptelea trifoliata* 'Aurea')	Small tree or large shrub, deciduous with a spreading habit, to 5m (16'). Young leaves are bright yellow, becoming greener with age.	Full sun to partial shade, well-drained soils of all kinds.
Bird cherry (*Prunus padus*)	From Europe and Asia. Large, deciduous tree that can reach 12m (40').	Sunny sites with moist, well-drained soils of all types. Waterlogging tolerant.
Laurel (*Prunus laurocerasus*)	Fast-growing, hardy, evergreen tree with dense canopy. Reaches up to 5m (16') but can be pruned to size.	Sun, partial shade or deep shade cast by large trees.
Portuguese laurel (*Prunus lusitanica*)	Large, evergreen reaching 15m (49'). Dark green leaves with red stems. Ideal for hedging and wind breaks.	Hardy. Full sun to shade, tolerates all soils except shallow chalk. Copes with dry, partial shade
Callery pear (*Pyrus calleryana* 'Chanticleer')	Deciduous, conical-shaped tree to 12m (40') over 20 years, with good autumn colour. Resilient species for large gardens.	Sunny aspect with well-drained soil. Drought tolerant.
Holm oak (*Quercus ilex*)	Mediterranean. Large, evergreen oak, growing to 25m (82').	Tolerant of a wide range of growing conditions. Copes well with drought.
Willows (Kilmarnock, pussy, white, red-stemmed etc) (*Salix* sp.)	Fast-growing deciduous trees, reaching between 5 and 15m (16 and 49'), but can be coppiced or pollarded. Adaptable and hardy trees. Can create a useful shelter belt for exposed gardens and orchards. Red-stemmed and pussy willow can grow to 20m (66'), while Kilmarnock willow grows to just 5m (16').	Prefers a sunny aspect on well-drained, moist soil of all types. Waterlogging tolerant.
Bald or swamp cypress (*Taxodium distichum*)	From the Everglades, USA. Large pyramidal-shaped deciduous conifer that drops its needles in autumn. A tree for large spaces as it grows to 25+m (82'). Good autumn colour.	Sun and partial shade. Tolerant of wind and waterlogging. When in waterlogged ground the tree sends up roots above ground called knees to take up oxygen.
Laurustinus (*Viburnum tinus*)	Not a tree, but a large winter-flowering evergreen shrub, 3mx3m (10x10'), produces fruits in autumn. Can be grown as a shelterbelt or hedge.	Hardy. Full sun or partial shade, moist well-drained soil. Can grow in deep shade against fence or wall and copes with dry partial shade. Wind resistant

What about autumn colours?

One of the delights of autumn is the change in leaf colour. For many gardeners, autumn colour is a factor when choosing trees and shrubs for the garden, while in parts of North America, it's a major tourist attraction. So how will climate change affect autumn colour?

In New England, leaves start to change colour from mid-September and reach a peak in mid-October. It is such big business that there are foliage maps and hotlines to ring to help you see the best colours available. Each year is different and estimates of peak colour are based on the temperatures and rainfall of summer. A cooler summer will delay leaf changes, while a hot, dry summer will bring it forward. A wetter-than-usual summer delays the colour, but it will be brighter. However, too much rain, with floods and waterlogged soils, stresses the trees and the leaves change colour early.

Now climate change is pushing back the date of peak colour. Studies show that between 1982 and 2008 the start of autumn had been delayed by more than nine days and its likely to reach two weeks in the near future. Not only will colour change be later, but experts predict that an early spring combined with a drier, hotter summer and an extended growing season into autumn will result in more muted colours overall.

Autumn colours are formed from pigments in the leaf. There are three main pigments; chlorophyll (green), carotenes (yellow) and anthocynanins (red), with chlorophyll masking the presence of the other pigments so leaves appear green. In autumn, the shorter days and cooler nights initiate the breakdown of chlorophyll so the green colour disappears and the carotenes become visible, turning the leaf yellow and orange. In preparation for leaf fall, a corky layer forms across the leaf stalk and this stops sugar from being moved out of the leaf. Instead, it gets converted to anthocyanins and the leaf takes on a red to pink appearance.

If autumn is warm, leaves continue to photosynthesise even though the sun is low in the sky and the days are shorter, but they produce less sugar. Not only is the autumn colour delayed until October or November, but less sugar means less anthocyanin and muted colours. A wet, cold summer also leads to poorer colour as the trees have produced less sugar. If spring is early and the summer dry, the leaves will have been very stressed and trees are likely to drop their leaves early before the colour changes are complete.

Left: The wonderful colours of fall in the USA

THE FLOWER GARDEN

Our gardens are going to look very different in 10 or 20 years time. That sounds a long way off, but for a garden it's not, especially when you consider it can take several years to get borders looking good. And with the extreme weather, getting plants established may be more difficult, so we'll have to get used to having more failures alongside our successess. It is definitely going to be a period of trial and error to see what works and what doesn't and adapting to the changes that will keep on coming as the country gets warmer and warmer. You will find increasingly that plants that we were told would never survive in this country will do very well, while some of our favourites may find conditions tough.

Imagine a quintessential English garden and you probably think of lush herbaceous borders, densely planted to give a riot of colour, set off against a backdrop of hedges, shrubs, specimen trees and a beautiful lawn. But what makes it so distinctive is the sheer diversity of plants we use in our gardens – trees, shrubs, herbaceous perennials, biennials, annuals, roses, climbers, grasses and bulbs. And it's this diversity that will help us as we move

Left: A cottage garden with a mix of flower types

into more uncertain gardening times. We may not be able to grow all our favourites in the decades ahead, but we may be able to capture the 'look' with a different selection of plants. A popular mantra is 'right plant, right place' but now we need to rethink the right place bit in its entirety!

The next decade may be tricky

When you are buying new plants for the garden, replanting a bed or establishing a new feature, try to choose species that will thrive into the future and group them according to their needs. Where possible, choose tough, drought-resistant perennials, trees and shrubs that will be able to cope with the drier summer conditions. The more-demanding plants will need extra care and water. Aim to create a resilient garden by knowing your plants and opt for some wild areas that encourage wildlife (see Chapter 6). Try to manage weeds and pests naturally rather than resorting to chemicals that will destroy the natural balance in your garden, especially in your soil. Also cut back on inputs such as fertilisers that not only encourage lush growth, but create a much needier outside space.

Do I choose frost-hardy plants?

We know that the chances of cold winters where temperatures fall to -10°C (14°F) or lower are going to become increasingly less

Tree ferns are not hardy, but don't like heat either

common, as are late spring frosts, but there is going to be the odd one that will catch you out. It may not be the occasional low temperatures that kill off your less-hardy plants, but a prolonged freeze or, more likely, a wet winter when a cold snap freezes already wet ground. So for the next few years, it will be best to play it safe by buying the hardier varieties, wrap up your valuable less-hardy-specimen plants, such as tree ferns and large palms, or move them under cover just in case.

A traditional border against a wall with a mix of species, some sun lovers, some not

The herbaceous border

The herbaceous border has its origins in the English cottage garden, with its mix of flowers for the vase and vegetables for the pot. It's a loose style of more natural planting using plants that vary in shape, colour and texture and that are at their best in summer. The most common element of the border is the herbaceous perennial – a hardy plant that dies down in the autumn, surviving underground and reappearing in spring when it produces a rapid growth of shoots and then flowers. Perennials are long-lived features of the border and as their performance wanes they can be rejuvenated by being dug up, split and replanted.

Traditional borders are likely to suffer as many of our favourite plants have lush growth and require a plentiful supply of water, making many of them distinctly unsuited to the warmer conditions of the future. Some of our regulars can cope with a summer drought, asters, phlox, lupins for example, but others, like bearded irises, love the heat but hate cold, wet winter weather. However, a warmer spring may mean there is less risk of losing delphiniums to late frost.

One problem with our borders is the way we mix up the planting. We tend to plant for colour or appearance and muddle up the water-hungry plants with the drought-tolerant ones. We won't be able to get away with that in the future. Our borders will have to be planted with water requirements firmly at the front of our mind.

Don't worry, it's still going to be possible to have an eye-catching herbaceous border, but the composition of species will be different. You may lose your favourites, but there will still be a huge range of herbaceous plants on offer, and most are quick and easy to establish, so unlike trees, you can redesign a herbaceous bed and see the effect in a few years. If you live in South East England, start thinking about plants that like a drier climate, may be more typical of France or even the Mediterranean, while gardeners in northern England and Scotland will be able to grow plants more typical of a Kentish garden.

Maintenance of borders is going to be important. If you are replanting a border or establishing a new one, take time to prepare the soil. Mulch heavily to suppress weeds, improve drainage and retain moisture. If the soil is heavy or the garden prone to waterlogging, raise the soil level. This will take a lot of effort and expense to bring in compost or soil, but it will pay off in the end. A raised bed is a good option too, as it will have better drainage and long-term survival for your plants.

Often herbaceous borders are left to their own devices when it comes to watering the garden, but you will have to pay more attention in a hot summer, especially if you have newly-established plants. And as mentioned before, drench the borders so you only have to water every few weeks, to encourage deep rooting. You may need to pay more attention to staking due to the greater likelihood of strong winds and heavy summer downpours. Winter storms and heavy rain may result in nutrients being washed out the soil, so an annual mulching will help to retain moisture and supply nutrients.

The backbone of the climate change border will be drought-tolerant perennials. Look for the easy-to-grow, low-maintenance species that flower well and, most importantly, are resilient. A colourful, long-lasting border could comprise: astilbe, eryngium, gaillardia, helenium, Jerusalem sage, lamb's-ear, mullein, scabious, black-eyed Susan, red hot poker, verbena, woodland sage and yarrow (see the Appendix for more ideas).

This drought-tolerant border in the Roads Water Smart Garden in Colorado, USA is only watered once or twice a year if needed.

Also, don't forget that tender perennials will come into their own in the future. These are plants such as arctotis, argyranthemum, asclepia, astroemeria, diascia, guara, heliotrope and penstemon. Compared with the traditional perennials, such as delphiniums and lupins, these warmer-climate perennials flower for many months; starting early and continuing into autumn. Already gardeners are finding that these tender perennials can overwinter, and with winters getting milder, overwintering will become the norm. You just have to guard against cold, wet soil.

Annuals can be planted in borders too, especially when the border is newly planted and there are gaps. Gazania and osteospermum

Now might be the time to think about incorporating pelargoniums into the border, rather than growing them in pots.

rain to percolate down to the water table, so the ground is less likely to get waterlogged and importantly, plants that like it dry are not sitting with wet roots in winter. In summer, the gravel acts as a mulch to retain moisture.

To be successful, a gravel garden needs to be prepared properly as it's not going to be watered or fed, beyond establishment. Many will say simply to clear away the grass to bare soil, add a weed barrier and a thick mulch of gravel, perhaps with a few rocks as a feature. However, time spent improving the soil will be invaluable, especially if the soil is compacted. Dig the soil over and incorporate plenty of organic matter and, if heavy, some grit. A good option is spent mushroom compost that is moisture-retaining, but light. Don't forget that there are a wide choice of gravels available, varying in colour and size and some that are self-binding too. To plant, scrape away gravel, dig out a hole, remove soil, place root ball and push back the gravel to leave a clean surface.

There are many drought-resistant plants suited to the dry conditions of a gravel garden. Gravel planting needs to be bright as paler, pastel colours can look a bit insipid against gravel. Some of the plants suited to this type of garden include cistus, euphorbia, lavender, nepeta and stachys, plus grasses to give texture and movement to the planting. And if you want to create an exotic style you don't have to look much further than agave, dasylirion and yucca.

cope well with heat and wind, while the fast-growing antirrhinum, petunia, pot marigold, and salpiglossis will all provide colour for many weeks.

A gravel garden

If you find the maintenance of a needy lawn too much hassle, why not dig it up and replace it with a gravel garden? Gravel helps heavy

A herb and gravel garden in Essex

The best place to visit for inspiration is the Beth Chatto garden in Essex. The garden was established in the 1990s on an old carpark and despite being located in one of the driest parts of the UK, it has never been watered. Beth Chatto explained that she wanted to make pictures with form, structure and colour. She tended to plant in triangles, varying the height of the plants and incorporating plenty of texture by contrasting spiky with soft. The use of accent colours and architectural plants through the planting would draw the eye.

The half-hardy annuals

Hardy annuals typically peak in mid-summer, so are more likely to suffer from lack of water in a hot year and run to seed, rather like some vegetable crops. Instead, in the future, it may be wise to look to the half-hardy annuals,

Salvias

Salvias are generally drought-resistant and long-flowering and many have scented foliage, plus they are great for attracting pollinators. They are the perfect option for a hot, dry border with free-draining soil. There are annual, biennial and perennial salvias. Planted in the right spot, the shrubby and hardy herbaceous salvias can overwinter. The half-hardy species need protection from frost, so are either grown in pots or lifted and moved to a greenhouse, for example eyelash sage (*Salvia blepharophylla*), Guatemalan leaf sage (*Salvia cacaliifolia*), pineapple sage (*Salvia rutulans*) and bog sage (*Salvia uliginosa*), while the gentian sage (*Salvia patens*) has tubers and can be mulched or lifted like a dahlia. Some of the popular annual salvias, including mealy cup sage (*Salvia farinacea*) and scarlet sage (*Salvia splendens*) are actually short-lived tender perennials and will survive winter if given protection.

including cleome, cobaea, cosmos, nicotinia, and tagetes. With warmer springs and reduced risk of late frost, they can be sown earlier. They could even be sown in autumn, like a hardy annual, as winters become milder. There may be opportunities to have an extra bedding season too, running from late summer through autumn into early winter, providng even more colour in the garden.

Prairie planting

Rather than a traditional herbaceous border, a drought-tolerant alternative is the free-form prairie-style planting, with drifts of grasses and perennials, all differing in shape, colour and flowering times. It provides interest year round with lots of movement, layers and view-points, but it's not an easy option and can be high maintenance!

The best location is one that is sunny all day, with soil that's rich in organic matter and well drained. Build up the soil to ensure good drainage and start with as few weeds as possible as these beds are notoriously difficult to weed once they are established. One way is to cover the bed with plastic for a year before planting to kill the weeds. Couch grass is particularly problematic, as it is in traditional herbaceous beds. The prairie-style planting works on all sizes of bed and can be planted with established container-grown plants or sown from seed, which creates a truly natural look, albeit more difficult to achieve. It's

A modern prairie garden

The Hauser and Wirth Garden in Somerset was designed by Piet Oudolf and has plenty of visual impact. This perennial meadow is a mix of grasses and perennial herbaceous plants that create a moving backdrop and amongst them is a selection of focus plants that add colour and texture. Colour in spring comes from bulbs, such as allium and camassia, but the perennial planting is at its best in late summer and early autumn. The soil has been mounded up and is gritty to improve drainage.

Drifts of helenium and anemone

important to keep the planting well-watered for the first year; these plants may be drought tolerant, but you want good establishment and for them to develop an extensive root system. Any gaps can be planted up with annuals. On-going maintenance involves mulching to both retain moisture and suppress weeds. Don't tidy the beds in autumn, but leave the old stalks to provide interest, frost protection, seed for birds and to help with drainage. They can be cut back in spring, once the weather is kinder. There is a list of suitable species in the Appendix and you can get ideas from the planting at Hauser and Wirth (see panel).

Can I grow bulbs?

Our gardens can look simply wonderful in spring with swaths of bulbs, from the first snowdrops to daffodils and tulips. But how will bulbs cope in a warmer world? Simply put, there are winners and losers.

Bulbs are storage organs. They enable plants to survive overwinter and reappear each year. These perennial plants build up food stores in their bulb during the summer months and then lie dormant through winter until the right conditions return. Some species are found in woodlands and they emerge early

The dry garden at Hyde Hall

The RHS Garden at Hyde Hall is in Essex, one of the driest parts of England and, believe it or not, the annual rainfall here is 61cm (24"), less than that of Rome. Construction of the dry garden started in 2001 to show gardeners that it's possible to have a beautiful garden that doesn't need watering. The garden lies on a south-facing slope and was created with mounds of hardcore and subsoil covered with a gritty topsoil and finished with gabbro boulders and a thick mulch of rounded flint. Its dry environment is very reminiscent of a Mediterranean hillside. Being on a hillside the plants are exposed to cold winds from the east and there's little shade from the sun and it's not been watered since its establishment. There are more than 400 different species, all perfectly at home in the dry environment, including agave, brachyglottis, giant viper's bugloss, euphorbias, perovskia, santolina, verbena and grasses, such as pampas grass, *Calamagrostis* and stipa. There are lots of self-seeded annuals too, including eryngiums, Californian poppies and nigella.

so they can complete their lifecycle before the tree leaves open and reduce the light reaching the ground. In the dry climates of the Mediterranean and South Africa, bulbs appear in spring or autumn to avoid the heat and drought of summer. A spring-flowering bulb doesn't respond to day length, but to the temperature, the size of the bulb and its food reserves. In bulbs like daffodils and tulips, development starts after flowering is complete in spring and early summer. In contrast, in summer bulbs, such as lilies and gladioli, the flower forms after the emergence of its shoot in spring and early summer.

Daffodils

In recent years, mild winter weather has resulted in daffodils flowering as early as December in Cornwall. But in 2010, there were no daffodils to be seen in March across the country – a late spring had led to a dearth of flowers and people were even asked to tweet any sightings. The reason for this variation

Daffodils don't like waterlogged soil

energy to reach the surface before their leaves can emerge and start to photosynthesise and replenish food stores.

Tulips

Tulips are a huge tourist attraction in some parts of the world and, if they flower too early, tourists will miss the flowers. The Tulip Time Festival in Holland, Michigan in the USA is a popular festival. In 1920, the festival started in mid-May, and this was the same until the mid-1970s, but then the trend to early flowering got underway. Now, the festival opens at the beginning of May, two weeks earlier than in the 1970s. If the weather is warm in February and March, rather than cold or wet, the flowering period of the tulips is much reduced, so there is plenty to concern the organisers.

Tulips, like the crocus and hyacinth, need a period of cold to stimulate flowering. This is called vernalisation. Tulips grow in mountainous areas with a temperate climate, such as Central Asia. Because of the cold winters, the tulip's development is triggered by temperature and, if the winter is mild and wet, tulips simply do not perform well.

Temperature is key in the life cycle of the tulip. It needs warmth to start developing the flower, and a period of cold to break dormancy and trigger the growth of the stem and flower in spring. If the temperatures are higher than average in spring, the quality of the flowers the following year can be adversely affected. The

is the winter temperature. It determines if flowers appear early or late.

Daffodils come from Spain and Portugal, so can cope with a mild winter. They grow in most soils and need plenty of organic matter to supply nutrients, but they don't like being waterlogged. If our winters get wetter and you have clay soils, daffodils will have to be planted where soil is well drained or in raised beds with sharp sand. They shouldn't be planted too deep as they have to expend more

The late flowering *Tulipa tarda* that is ideal for naturalising

bulbs will be at a more advanced stage when they are harvested and put into storage and this leads to the dehydration of the flower bud.

As temperatures increase and winters become milder, it will become more difficult to grow crocus, tulip and hyacinth because of the lack of chill factor, but they could be grown in a climate change garden if they are given 6 to 8 weeks of chill to trigger the flowering cycle. To overcome this hurdle, it may be we end up popping our tulips in a fridge for a couple of months early in winter and planting them out in January or that we start buying pre-chilled bulbs.

Can I still grow tulips?

What can you do if you want to grow tulips? One option is to plant them in shady places so they are less affected by unseasonally-warm weather. Once the tulips have experienced some cold weather, or when the ground temperature has fallen, mulch heavily to maintain the cool conditions. Another way forward may be to plant a range of bulbs with differing rates of maturation so there are better chances of some flowering. There are lots of different species and varieties of tulips and some will be better suited to a warmer garden than others. Amongst the best-suited are the Darwin hybrids that were developed by Lefeber in Holland. They produce a single, large flower on a long, sturdy stem. These mid-to-late spring tulips flower for up to five years and are good for naturalising (see below). Another option is to choose late-flowering varieties, such as Queen of the Night, Menton, Dreamland, and Dordogne, but their flowering period may be shortened if early spring is dry and warm.

Naturalised bulbs

The modern bulb has been bred to deliver a great display in the first and second year, and then be replaced, while tulips grown for cut flowers are kept for just one year and then discarded. However, there are naturalised bulbs - the daffodils, crocus and snowdrops that are true perennials and have been selected for their ability to reappear year after year. Tulips can be naturalised too, but you have to choose varieties that have been bred to naturalise or use species of tulips, such as *Tulipa clusiana* and *Tulipa tarda*, that will last many years and multiply. Being perennials, naturalised bulbs have a chance to adapt to the changing climate.

Bulbs for a warmer climate

Rather than attempt to grow daffodils and tulips in the future, it may be better to switch to bulbs that are adapted to a warmer climate with dry summers and mostly mild winters with lowest temperatures around -5°C. The options include:

Narcissi They originated in the Mediterranean and can cope with summer drought as the bulb is dormant in the ground. However, they are more susceptible to wet winters with waterlogged, cold soil, as this will delay flowering.

Alliums These bulbs flower from spring to summer. They are planted in autumn, deep in a fertile soil to give a good flowering for many years. They like full sun, but don't like cold, wet soils or exposed conditions. Some can naturalise in grassland, for example, *Allium hollandicum*, while others such as *Nectaroscordum siculum* can be found in light woodland where the soil stays moist, but not waterlogged, and the bulbs are sheltered from the worst of late winter and early spring weather. They are a good option to plant in the herbaceous border to give early interest.

Summer snowflake This produces spikes of bell flowers in mid-spring and is dormant in summer. It is planted in autumn in a moist, fertile soil, well drained in sunny to light shade. It can cope with boggy areas, so could be planted around ponds and in bog gardens. It naturalises easily and looks great under trees.

Woodland anemone This hardy bulb has long-lasting daisy-like blue, white or pink flowers. It flowers early, has a long season and naturalises well. It likes partial shade with fertile, well-drained soil, but will cope with full sun. It's ideal under deciduous trees and shrubs.

Spanish vs English bluebells

In 2008, English bluebells were recorded flowering in February rather than April and May. Studies suggest that this species is sensitive to spring temperatures and it will come into flower or leaf between 3 and 8 days earlier for every 1°C increase in temperature. It was named as one of the four UK species most likely to struggle with climate change, the others being garlic mustard, larch and sycamore, while the wood anemone was highlighted as one that might do well.

The Spanish bluebell was introduced to gardens in the late 17th century. It's a vigorous garden plant that produces scentless, pale blue flowers with paler stripes. The bells fall in all directions around the stem, rather than drooped to one side as with the native bluebell (right). It has become naturalised in hedgerows, woodlands and parks and spreads quickly. Climate change suits it, so it's spread is likely to continue as the temperatures rise.

Other options include plants with tubers and rhizomes rather than bulbs. They include:

Agapanthus or African lily. This rhizomatous perennial is a native to South Africa. It is planted in autumn or early spring to flower from summer to autumn. It's drought and salt-tolerant, so ideal for seaside gardens. It needs a fertile, well-drained soil and can be protected from cold weather by a thick mulch in winter, but the less hardy types in containers need to be moved under cover.

Bearded or German iris This is a rhizomatous perennial from Eastern Mediterranean, which likes full sun. It should be planted in a south-facing border with a well-drained soil, but it doesn't like waterlogged soil.

Pineapple lily These eye-catching plants with

Containers of pineapple lilies

a spike of star-shaped flowers are usually growing in containers, but in a warmer garden they could be planted in a sunny border. Pick an open sunny spot with fertile, well-drained soil. They can tolerate drought, but this will adversely affect the flowers, so don't let them dry out. In winter, mulch with bark or straw or lift the bulbs and store in a greenhouse

Crinum or swamp lily This produces beautiful funnel-shaped flowers held above the leaves. It needs full sun and a well-drained soil that doesn't get waterlogged in winter. It may need protection against frost in northern areas. It's ideal for sunny beds along a wall, with the bulb planted so the neck just emerges from the soil.

Nerine An easy-to-grow late-flowering bulb from South Africa that needs a sunny location with well-drained, gritty soil. It's intolerant of waterlogging and wet soils in winter, so plant bulbs with their neck just above the surface of the soil. Flower stalks appear in autumn. An ideal position is at the bottom of a sunny wall. These hardy plants benefit from some water when growing, but can be dry when dormant.

A succulent hanging basket

Hanging baskets are usually very demanding of water and in a hot summer there is a need to water them daily. So a new twist on the hanging basket is to use succulents. Not only will the hanging basket be low maintenance, but it will provide year-round interest. All you need to do is water occasionally in drier weather, don't water from late autumn to spring and give them a feed once in spring.

Succulents

Succulents are adapted to living in desert and arid habitats where there is little water and thin soils. They store water in their fleshy leaves, stems and roots, while the waxy layer covering their leaves and stems reduces any water loss, helping them conserve water. They tick all the boxes – easy to grow, drought resilient, evergreen and low maintenance, so expect to see more of them in gardens in the future. Their drought resistance makes them the ideal choice for a green roof or vertical garden too.

Succulents need a sunny site and they can cope with low temperatures. Deserts can be incredibly cold by night but, like many of the heat-loving plants mentioned in this chapter, they can't cope with waterlogging or wet soil

in winter. If they get too wet, they will be killed by frost and snow. The right conditions can be achieved by planting them in pots, containers or gravel beds. They grow well at the foot of sunny walls as the wall radiates heat and helps to shield them from rain.

There are places in the UK where succulents grow profusely, not least the fabulous gardens of Michael's Mount on the Cornish coast. Here the mild climate and exposed, rocky site is perfect for growing a subtropical flora. Frosts are rare as the rocks act as huge storage heaters, absorbing heat during the day and releasing it at night. In summer, temperatures exceed 40°C. The cliffs are planted with an array of succulents including agave, aeonium, aloe, sedums plus other exotics including ginger lilies, leucodendrum and coronilla.

Left: The eye-catching Aeonium or tree houseleek

Succulents to consider

Succulent	Characteristics
Aloe	Various types, including *Aloe vera* and *Aloe variegata*. Easy to grow with long fleshy leaves and toothed margins. Spikes of tubular yellow – orange flowers. Needs a sunny location and to be moved to a frost-free location in winter, so ideal for containers. Good for coastal and urban gardens.
Houseleeks (*Sempervivum*)	These rosette-forming succulents are very easy, tough and slow growing. Their summer flowers are good for pollinators. They are the extreme survivors, coping with high temperatures and drought, as well as being hardy. They can be planted in pots, bricks, walls and gravel gardens as they can grow in very little compost.
Mexican snowball (*Echeveria elegans*)	Rounded, rosette-forming plants with pointed leaves, upright stems and pink-coral coloured flowers in late winter and spring. Plant in full sun in a southerly, sheltered aspect. Not hardy.
Stonecrop (*Sedum*)	There are various kinds of sedums including the ground cover types, such as *Sedum acre,* that are used on green roofs and the taller *Sedum spectabile, Sedum telephium* and the hybrid *Sedum* 'Matrona'. The taller clump-forming succulents have fleshy leaves and stems, but they do have a tendency to collapse if they are given too much water. They need harsh conditions to create a sturdy growth. Plant in a sunny spot in well drained soil. They are drought tolerant and work well with grasses, agapanthus, eryngium and salvia. They don't like waterlogged or wet soils.
Tree houseleek (*Aeonium*)	Striking, upright succulent with rosettes of leaves in a range of colours from green to bronze and black. *Aeonium* 'Zwartkop' is a particularly eye-catching plant with deep black-purple leaves and small yellow flowers. Aeoniums are great for courtyard gardens and frost-free locations. They need a sunny, sheltered position in summer, for example near south-facing wall, but they are not frost hardy or tolerant of wet feet. In winter, move them to a cool conservatory or porch. They drop their older leaves in winter so if they start to look leggy, the top of the shoot can be cut off and rooted in gritty compost and the rest of the plant repotted and allowed to reshoot.

Can I have a lawn?

Many say that a garden is not a garden without a lawn, but it's going to be the first to suffer in the climate change garden. The more highly managed and manicured the lawn, the quicker it's going to suffer. We are going to have to get used to our lawns turning yellow and then brown in a dry summer, but despite the horrible appearance, grass is a truly resilient plant and will recover within weeks. Just remember 'brown is the new green'!

Grasses are the dominant plants of the savannah and prairies, supporting millions of grazing animals. They are tough plants with deep roots that extend metres into ground to reach water. The roots stabilise the soil and help to build up a humus-rich earth that supports high productivity. The prairies experience a continental climate – hot dry summers, cold winters – so grasses and other plants can cope with months of hot, dry weather with the occasional storm, something to remember when we think about the future of our garden lawn.

Our lawns comprise a mix of grasses. Fine-leaved grasses are used to create the pristine, manicured lawn that requires mowing, feeding, weeding, spiking and watering as soon as its dry. This type of lawn will be the first to suffer in a drought or from flooding. A lawn with a selection of broad-leaved grasses is more tolerant of trampling and games of football. Generally, lawns can look after

Climate change and lawn mowers

While on the topic of lawns, think about your climate change credentials. How much fuel do you use to cut the lawn? The best climate-friendly option is not to cut your lawn and have a flower meadow instead! Next best is the push lawnmower. These are much improved design-wise and they have the added benefit of affording a good work out too, with all the pushing involved.

After that you might consider the recycler or mulching lawnmower. This mower chops up the grass clippings and drops them on the lawn to decompose and recycle the nutrients. They are efficient energy-wise as they reduce the time taken to cut the lawn by as much as half, so there is less fuel used per mow. There are some cordless mowers powered by lithium-ion batteries, so although they require electricity to recharge them, it's more efficient than using a petrol engine, especially if the electricity is supplied by renewable energy sources.

Don't worry if your lawn turns brown

the cut so that their leaves are left with more leaf, as a low cut will weaken them. A long cut will also leave the grasses better placed to recover after rain. Also, don't collect the clippings. Instead, leave them on the surface as a mulch to reduce water evaporation from the soil, but be careful that the clippings themselves are not too long, as if so, they will potentially smother (and cause damage to) the lawn rather than mulching to its benefit.

A summer drought often ends with a heavy downpour, which can lead to flooding, waterlogging and compaction. In these conditions, stay off the wet grass as this can cause compaction.

Warmer temperatures mean a longer growing season. The downside means that lawns have to be mowed for longer, from early spring to late autumn, and in the mildest areas lawns hay have to be mown all year round. Weeds will benefit too. Moss likes to grow in spring before the grass becomes active, so warmer winters may result in moss growing for longer, but the grass will start to grow earlier too, so this may be enough to counter the moss growth.

Wet winter care

Lawns suffer just as much, if not more, in winter. Heavy rain combined with heavy foot traffic can leave the lawn a muddy mess, especially those on less well-drained soils, clay or compacted ground. The wet conditions

themselves as grasses spring back into life once the rain returns. The lawn may not look attractive but it really doesn't need watering.

The higher temperatures will favour different grasses. The finer-leaved grasses are the least tolerant of drought, while grasses with tough fibrous leaves are better suited. So, annual meadow grass (*Poa annua)* and fescues (*Festuca spp.*) will lose out to bentgrass (*Agrostis tenuis),* while some of the weeds will be winners too, especially clover and yarrow. And looking far ahead it is likely that by 2050, we will need to be growing those grasses typical of southern Europe or Florida!

Lawn care during a drought

If you simply have to mow your lawn during a drought, you can help the grasses by raising encourage mosses, lichens and algae to thrive. While the soil is waterlogged, stay off it to avoid further damage. A quick fix is to overseed the damaged areas. Once it stops raining and the soil has dried enough to be worked and has warmed up for seed to germinate, rake the surface and expose the soil a little, sprinkle over seed and tread in lightly. Job done!

There are remedial actions you can take if your soil is prone to waterlogging. In autumn, you can improve it by forking, spiking or slitting and then filling the holes or slits with sand to aid the percolation of water through the soil. This can also be done after waterlogging and flooding, but wait for the water to drain away.

A very badly-drained lawn may not recover from flooding as the standing water penetrates into the soil, pushing out the oxygen, and creating anaerobic conditions around the roots, so the plants die. It may be better to start afresh by improving the soil, adding layer of sharp sand and topsoil to improve drainage and either re-turf or seed.

Ornamental grasses

You may get rid of the lawn, but there's no reason why you can't grow ornamental grasses which are just as drought resilient as their lawn grass cousins. A wide range of grasses are suited to a hot dry border: African fountain grass, fescue, Japanese blood grass, marram

A shady corner is perfect for warmer summers

grass, Mexican feather grass, New Zealand wind grass, pampas grass, sedge and switch grass.

What can I grow for a warmer summer?

Looking ahead, you can think subtropical and Mediterranean. The Exotic Garden at Great Dixter in Sussex has the appearance of a tropical jungle with its lush foliage and dense planting. In 1992, Christopher Lloyd and Fergus Garrett removed the rose beds that were suffering from replant disease and planted large-leaved foliage plants, such as dahlia, canna, papyrus, and hardy Japanese banana. One of the restrictions on the choice of plant was hardiness. Those selected were hardy and capable of surviving a cold winter, but as our

A dry, gravel garden with rows of lavender

climate warms up this type of planting can be supplemented with a greater range of subtropicals, such as agave, banana, palm, ginger, abutilon and even pineapple.

Protecting tender exotics

With extreme cold becoming less common, especially in the south of the UK, it may be easy to get complacent and not bother to protect the less hardy of your plants over winter. The best approach is to make sure any borderline exotics are wrapped up for winter.

Some plants can be surprisingly resilient, the hardy banana for example, is pretty tough and it can grow back after losing its leaves to cold and frost due to having hardy roots. Cordylines also have resilient roots and will regrow from the base of the stem. It can take until early summer for these to appear so don't give up too soon. Tree ferns may become more common in gardens as winters become milder, but give them protection, especially the growing points and you will find they can cope with temperatures down to -10C (14°F), while the windmill palm will survive

Right: Great Dixter in Sussex

Masses of pink bracts of bougainvillea

the extreme cold of -17C (1.4°F). Interestingly, many of these plants get hardier once they are established, so if you can get them through their first years as they put down their roots, you should have more luck.

Growing bougainvillea

The archetypal plant of the Mediterranean has to be the bougainvillea, so can we grow it in the UK?

Bougainvillea is an evergreen climber that always seems to be covered in pink-purple bracts that surround the tiny white star-like flowers. However, this plant cannot cope with frost and temperatures dipping below -3°C (26°F). Despite that, people are successfully growing it outside all year round in London, Devon and Cornwall, and even in coastal regions of Sussex, so it won't be many years before those living in the south of the UK will be able to grow them outside too. For those living in areas where there is too great a risk of frost, the best way to grow bougainvillea is in a large pot as a standard or espalier and keep it outside in summer and in a greenhouse or conservatory in winter. If you are planting it outside, you need a sunny, protected spot that is frost free, so a sheltered urban garden or under an overhang of a south-facing wall would be ideal. Temperatures under 10°C (50°F) cause the plant to go deciduous.

A Mediterranean flora

Many parts of the world have a Mediterranean climate of hot, dry summers and mild, wet winters. As well as the Mediterranean basin itself, this climate is found in California, southern and southwestern Australia, Mexico, central Chile and South Africa, and each has their own characteristic assemblage of species adapted to the conditions. These plants tend to have silvery, needle-like or hairy leaves that reduce the surface area from which water can be lost and also reflect heat away from the leaf. The hairs help to trap any early morning dew too. Often the leaves are aromatic due to an oily film on the leaves that acts like a sunscreen. These plants usually have deep roots to reach down to the water table and survive drought. The fleshy-leaved species have a different survival strategy, they store water in their leaves and stems, while others have storage organs, such as tubers, bulbs or rhizomes, which enable the plant to survive underground during the dry season. Those typical of the dry slopes of the Mediterranean include achillea, artemisia, cerinthe, cistus, eryngium, lavender, nepeta, phlomis, rosemary, santolina, sage and thyme. From the arid habitats of North America come penstemon, dahlia, gaura and salvias, while the South African fynbos is home to agapanthus, crocosmia, dierama, kniphofia and protea.

There are different varieties of bougainvillea, and one of the hardiest and best suited for the UK is *Bougainvillea spectibilis* as it has a natural, cold-dormancy during which it needs to be kept as dry as possible. The plants often shed their leaves when the new growth starts in spring and then flowering occurs in summer. Bougainvilleas are vigorous climbers and you need to feed them to get the best colour. They can be given a high nitrogen feed from late spring onwards and watered if necessary. Once the bracts start to colour up you can switch to a high potassium feed. Although these plants like the heat, the colour is improved if the plant is given a bit of shade. The bracts will drop and then you can give more nitrogen feed to encourage a fresh flush of bracts. After the bracts have lost their colour you can cut the shoots back by about half to encourage new bract formation.

Creating your own Mediterranean garden

As dry summers with high temperatures and more sunshine hours become increasingly common, along with the lessening risk of late frost, there is an opportunity for gardeners in the southern half of the UK to grow plants more usual of the Mediterranean region.

What's typical of a Mediterranean garden?

Certainly, gravel paths with a backdrop of formal shapes created from trees and clipped hedges, contrasted with the irregular planting of drought-tolerant plants. Shade is key, both for people and plants, to survive the heat of the day, so imagine pergolas or trellis creating shady corners with seating surrounded by scrambling plants, such as vines, hops, jasmine or a scented rambling rose. Water, too, is typical of this style of garden; not just for the visual and sound effects, but to create humidity and provide wildlife with a source of water.

Mediterranean and subtropical plants are going to need a sunny spot and a well-drained soil, so ground preparation is important. Although we are great fans of no-dig, you need to get the soil right at the start, so mix in grit and organic matter to create the essential well-drained bed. But the soil doesn't need much by way of fertility as this will cause the plants to put on too much lush growth that is more susceptible to winter damage. It's bulk you want to boost moisture retention and drainage. Mulch with gravel too, to conserve as much water as possible. The gravel will also reflect heat, helping to keep the roots cool in a hot summer and suppress weeds. It also helps to keep water away from the base of the stems and that reduces the risk of rotting in winter.

Hard landscaping with gravel, cobbles, pebbles and rocks avoids the need for a lawn and creates an opportunity for a beautiful gravel garden. Raised beds will give a good depth of well-drained soil enabling plants to keep their roots dry in winter. If you have a sloping garden with a sunny aspect you could build a terraced gravel garden with a series of low retaining walls down the slope to create that Mediterranean-hillside look. This would warm up quickly, as well as be free draining. Make sure you have a drainage point at the bottom of a retaining wall, so water can pass through and not collect.

Terracotta pots create a typical Mediterranean look and allow you to grow specimen plants that can cope with high summer temperatures, but need protection from the cold and wet in winter, like lemon and lime trees, olives or typical shrubs, such as oleander and frangipani.

Lavender loves the heat in summer

Specimen lemon trees in large pots

Succulents and herbs surrounded by gravel

Planting ideas for a Mediterranean garden

Statement plants	Agapanthus, agave, canna, cordyline, fan palm (*Chamaerops humilis*), phoenix palm (*Phoenix canariensis*), and Chusan palm (*Trachycarpus fortunei*), Ethiopian banana (*Ensete ventricosum*), fig (*Fatsia japonica*), New Zealand flax (*Phormium sp.*) and yucca. The more risky species can be planted in large containers unless you live in a frost-free zone, but some of the hardier ones can go out all year in borders.
Aromatic, sun-loving evergreen herbs	There are many to choose from, including bay, lavender, rosemary, sage and thyme. Plant them near seating and path edges so visitors brush up against them and release the scent.
Shrubs	Options include bottlebrush, broom, ceanothus, choisya, cistus, euphorbia, grey-leaved euryops, hebe, hibiscus, rockrose, laurustinus, *Lomelmosia minoana* from Crete, olearia, osmanthus, perovskia, *Retama sphaerocarpa* from southern Spain, and santolina.
Sun-loving herbaceous perennials	Achillea, bear's breech, bugloss, centaurea, echinops, echium, eryngium, hoary mugwort, ice plant, Jerusalem sage, lamb's ear, lavatera, red hot poker, red valerian and salvia.
Grasses to soften the borders	African fountain grass, Mexican feather grass, miscanthus, New Zealand wind grass and switch grass.
Climbing plants	Creeping fig, crimson glory vine, grape vine, honeysuckle, Japanese wisteria, trumpet vine (some are hardy) and winter jasmine.
Plants for pots	Agave, aloe, bay tree, bougainvillea, lantana, lemon, olive, osteospermum and pelargonium.
Trees	Stone pine, Italian privet, Italian cypress and Portuguese laurel.
Bromeliads	*Fascicularia* and *Puya*.

Growing gingers

The Victorians grew the spectacular gingers (*Hedychium* sp.) in conservatories and since then they have been considered a house plant.

They may be tropical and subtropical plants, but they are far hardier than first thought and as our winters get milder, more are able to survive outside rather than be moved under cover. But you do have to select the right ginger. Also, it can be tricky to get some species to flower as they need long days, a long growing season and lots of heat, so many are disappointed when their ginger plant doesn't flower.

According to ginger expert Andrew Gaunt, who has the national collection of ornamental gingers, they are easy to look after. They range in height from just 30cm (12") to more than 2m (6'6") and bear the most amazing flower spikes. They need a warm spot, but it doesn't have to be in full sun, plus plenty of water when in full growth. They start growing in spring when temperatures rise above 10°C and continue to grow through summer until the first autumn frosts when the leaves die back and the rhizome overwinters in the ground undisturbed.

While the plants can cope with wet conditions in summer, they are intolerant of winter water-logging and the ground must not freeze solid. If you live in a colder area, the rhizomes can be protected with a thick mulch of straw with a piece of plastic pegged down over it to keep it in place.

The following species all grow and flower well in the milder parts of the country: *H.coccineum, H.chrysoleucum, H.densiflorum, H. forestii, H.gardnerianum, H.greenii* and *H.spicatum.* If you are worried about your overwintering conditions, grow the ginger in a pot and sink it into the ground in summer so you can lift it for winter without disturbing the roots. If overwintered inside, the ginger will stay evergreen throughout winter and flowering will be earlier.

APPENDIX

Plant hardiness

This is the ability of a plant to survive outside over winter. To help gardeners choose the right plant, organisations such as the Royal Horticultural Society (RHS) in the UK and the USDA in the USA give hardiness ratings to plants.

USDA Hardiness zones range from 1 to 13, 1 being the coldest zone, which experiences temperatures down to -50°F (Arctic) and 13 being the tropical zone. Each zone covers a range of 10°F which means the North American continent can be mapped in great

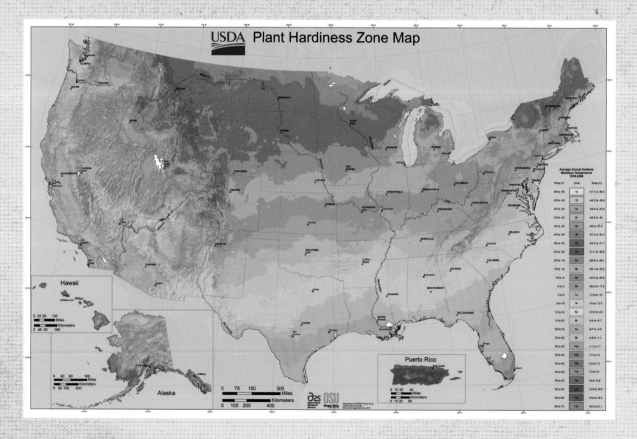

detail. Plants are given a zone according to the lowest temperature that they can withstand.

The RHS has a hardiness rating for the UK based on a plant's ability to withstand cold temperatures. It's not as detailed as the USA, as the range of climates is less extreme, but there is greater variation. It's based on minimum temperatures, ranging from H1a (heated greenhouse) to H7 (very hardy).

UK hardiness zone	
H1 Tropical	Best grown in a heated greenhouse that is warmer than 15°C (59°F) or as a house plant
H1b Subtropical	Should be grown in a heated greenhouse or indoors with minimum temperature of between 10 and 15°C (50 and 59°F)
H1c Warm temperate	Should be grown in a heated greenhouse, conservatory or as a house plant with a minimum temperature of between 5 to 10°C (41 to 50°F)
H2 Tender	Can be kept in a cool or frost-free greenhouse in winter at a minimum temperature of between 1 to 5°C (34 to 41°F)
H3 Half-hardy	Can be kept in an unheated greenhouse or outdoors in mild areas at a minimum temperature of between -5 to 1°C (23 to 34°F)
H4 Hardy	Can be kept outdoors during an average winter where the temperature gets to between -10 to -5°C (14 to 23°F)
H5 Hardy	Can be kept outdoors in a cold winter where the temperature falls to -15 to -10°C (5 to 14°F)
H6 Hardy	Can be kept outdoors in a very cold winter where the temperature falls to -20 to -15°C (-4 to 5°F)
H47 Very hardy	Will survive outdoors during the worst UK winters when temperatures may fall lower than -20°C (-4°F)

RESOURCES

To help you plan your own climate change garden we have put together a list of suppliers, books and other information that might prove useful.

Suppliers

Dalefoot Compost Dalefoot Farm, Heltondale, Penrith, CA10 2QL www.dalefootcomposts.co.uk Suppliers of a range of composts making use of local, sustainable materials, such as bracken and wood.

First Tunnels Altham, Lancashire. Suppliers of domestic and commercial polytunnels www.firsttunnels.co.uk

Green&Blue New Road, Perranporth, Cornwall, TR6 0DL https://greenandblue.co.uk.Suppliers of the innovative bee brick that is incorporated into buildings to create homes for mason bees.

Organic Gardening Catalogue https://www.organiccatalogue.com/ Our go-to place for organic seeds and other garden supplies. Garden Organic members get a discount.

Pennard Plants The Walled Gardens, Pennard, Somerset, BA46TP www.pennardplants.com Suppliers of one of the largest selections of edible plants and heritage seeds

Primrose 44 Portman Rd, Reading, Berkshire, RG301EA https://www.primrose.co.uk An online retailer supplying everything to do with the garden

Useful organisations

Garden Organic
Ryton Gardens, Wolston Lane, Coventry, CV8 3LG www.gardenorganic.org.uk Founded as the Henry Doubleday Research Association, Garden Organic promotes organic growing through campaigns, advice, community work and research.

Royal Horticultural Society (RHS)
80 Vincent Square, London. SW1P 2PE www.rhs.org.uk The UK's leading gardening charity that promotes horticulture through flower shows including the Chelsea Flower Show.

Soil Association
Spear House, Victoria Rd, Bristol, BS1 6AD www.soilassociation.org Charity campaigning for healthy, humane and sustainable food, farming and land use.

Further reading
Books by the authors
Living on One Acre or Less, Sally Morgan, Green Books, 2016

The Primrose Water Feature Book, Kim Stoddart, IPN, 2018

Other books and articles

Creating a Forest Garden, Martin Crawford Green Books, 2010

Gaia's Garden: A guide to home-scale permaculture, Toby Hemenway, Chelsea Green, 2009

Gardening in a changing climate, RHS in collaboration with the University of Sheffield and University of Reading, RHS, 2017. You can download the report: https://www.rhs.org.uk/science/gardening-in-a-changing-world/climate-change

Sepp Holzer's Permaculture: A practical guide for farms, orchards and gardens, Sepp Holzer, Permanent Publications, 2010

Teeming with microbes: The organic gardener's guide to the soil food web, Jeff Lowenfels and Wayne Lewis, Timber Press, revised 2010

The Holistic Orchard: Tree Fruits and Berries the Biological Way, Michael Phillips, Chelsea Green, 2012

The Impacts of Climate Change on Gardens in the UK, Richard Bisgrove and Professor Paul Hadley of the University of Reading (2002). Summarised by Dr Phil Gates, University of Durham 2002 UK Climate IMPACT Programme https://ukcip.ouce.ox.ac.uk/wp-content/PDFs/Gardens_summary.pdf

Plant lists

We have put together some suggestions for species that can grow in different places of the garden. These lists are just some of the many species to consider. We have more information on our website (www.climatechangegarden.com). Where possible we have given the common and Latin name of the plants, but in some cases there is no common name.

The tough shrubs

The following list of shrubs are tough and reliable. They are relatively common, unfussy species and one of the reasons they are grown widely is their ability to grow and thrive in a wide range of conditions. They may not be 'exciting' but form a reliable backbone to the garden and are relatively cheap to buy.

Buddleia (*Buddleja davidii*), cherry laurel (*Prunus laurocerasus*), *Cotoneaster horizontalis*, dogwood (*Cornus alba*), *Euonymus fortunei*, flowering currant (*Ribes sanguineum*), forsythia (*Forsythia x intermedia*), holly (*Ilex aquifolium*), Japanese quince (*Chaenomeles speciosa*), mahonia (*Mahonia aquifolium* and *Mahonia x media*), privet (*Ligustrum lucidum*), shrub rose (*Rosa glauca*) and laurustinus (*Viburnum tinus*).

Plants for wet soils

These are soils that are damp and drain poorly. Puddles may lie on the surface. In these types of wet areas, avoid plants that hate wet roots and go for plants that can cope. Many of the plants listed can cope with short-term flooding as well as waterlogging.

Perennials: Amsonia, astilbe (*Astilbe chinensis*), astrantia (*Astrantia major*), bergenia (*Bergenia cordifolia*), bistort (*Persicaria amplexicaulis*), black-eyed Susan (*Rudbeckia fulgida*), bloody crane's-bill (*Geranium sanguineum*), candelabra primula (*Primula candelabra*), cardinal flower (*Lobelia cardinalis*), daylily (*Hemerocallis*), elecampane (*Inula helenium*), *Eupatorium purpureum*, globe flower (*Trollius europeaus*), great burnet (*Sanguisorba officinalis*), *Gunnera manicata*, hosta, *Houttuynia cordata*, kaffir lily (*Schizostylis*), lady's smock (*Cardamine quinquefolia*), leopard plant (*Ligularia dentata*), Maltese cross (*Lychnis chalcedonica*), marsh marigold (*Caltha palustris*), meadow rue (*Thalictrum delavayi*), meadowsweet (*Filipendula ulmaria*), miscanthus, New Zealand flax (*Phormium tenax*), ornamental rhubarb (*Rheum palmatum*), purple loosestrife (*Lythrum salicaria*), plume thistle (*Cirsium rivulare*), rodgersia (*Rodgersia aesculifolia* and *R. pinnata*), royal fern (*Osmunda regalis*), sedge (*Carex*), Siberian iris (*Iris sibirica*), water avens (*Geum rivale*) and yellow loosestrife (*Lysimachia punctata*).

Shrubs: dogwood (*Cornus alba* and *C. sericea*), elder (*Sambucus racemosa*), firethorn (*Pyracantha*), guelder rose (*Viburnum opulus*), shrubby cinquefoil (*Potentilla fruticosa*) and spiraea (*Spiraea japonica*).

Trees: Alder (*Alnus glutinosa*) and the evergreen Italian alder (*A. cordata*), birch (*Betula nigra* and *B. pendula*), hornbeam (*Carpinus betulus*), poplar (*Populus*), rowan (*Sorbus aucuparia*), snowy mespilus (*Amelanchier lamarckii*), swamp cypress (*Taxodium distichum*) and willow (*Salix*).

Plants for the dry garden

These are plants that can cope with drier soils and periods of drought in summer. They tend not to like their roots wet in winter so need a well-drained soil.

Herbaceous border: African daisy (*Osteospermum*), bearded iris (*Iris germanica*), Californian fuchsia (*Zauschneria californica*), cardoon (*Cynara cardunculus*), catmint (*Nepeta sp.*), delosperma (*Delosperma cooperi*), evening primrose (*Oenothera biennis*), globe thistle (*Echinops sp.*), gaillardia (*Gaillardia x grandiflora*), ice plant (*Sedum spectabile*), lamb's ears (*Stachys byzantine*), lupin (*Lupinus arboreus*), milkweed (*Asclepias tuberosa*), mullein (*Verbascum nigrum*), penstemon, poppy (*Papaver*), red hot poker (*Kniphofia*), red-velvet sage (*Salvia confertiflora*), scabious (*Knautia macedonica*), sea holly (*Eryngium sp.*), spurge (*Euphorbia sp.*), verbena (*Verbena bonariensis*), wild indigo (*Baptisia australis*) and yarrow (*Achillea millefolium*).

Grasses: Blue fescue (*Festuca glauca*), fountain grass (*Pennisetum villosum, P. orientale)*, golden oats (*Stipa gigantea*), miscanthus (*Miscanthus sinesis*), pampas grass (*Cortaderia selloana*), switch grass (*Panicum virgatum*).

Small shrubs: Blackcurrant sage (*Salvia grahamii*), box (*Buxus sempervirens*), cape honeysuckle (*Tecoma capensis*), cotton lavender (*Santolina chamaecyparissus*), flowery senna (*Senna corymbosa*), heavenly bamboo (*Nandina domestica*), hebe, honey flower (*Melianthus major*), Jerusalem sage (*Phlomis fruticosa*), kerosene bush (*Ozothamnus hookeri*), lavender (*Lavandula sp.*), rock rose (*Helianthemum nummularium*), rosemary (*Rosmarinus officinalis*), Russian sage (*Perovskia atriplicifolia*), shrubby bindweed (*Convolvulus cneorum*), Spanish broom (*Spartium junceum*), St John's wort (*Hypericum perforatum*), sunrose (*Cistus x hybridus*) and wormwood (*Artemisia arborescens*)

Medium to large shrubs: Abelia (*Abelia x grandiflora*), bottle brush (*Callistemon citrinus*), broom (*Cytisus* 'Burkwoodii'), Californian lilac (*Ceanothus*), daisy bush (*Olearia macrodonta*), eleagnus (*Elaeagnus angustifolia*), evergreen laburnum (*Piptanthus nepalensis*), fremontodendron (*Fremontodendron californicum* 'California Glory'), juniper (*Juniperus communis*), oleander (*Nerium oleander*), tree poppy (*Romneya coulteri*) and yucca (*Yucca filamentosa*).

Climbers: Bluebell creeper (*Sollya heterophylla*), Chilean glory flower (*Eccremocarpus*), golden guinea flower (*Hibbertia scandens*), jasmine (*Jasminum officinale, Jasmine angulare* and *Jasminum azoricum*), passion flower (*Passiflora caerulea*), potato vine (*Solanum crispum*) and trumpet vine (*Campsis radicans*)

Plants for dry shade

Astrantia (*Astrantia major*), barrenwort (*Epimedium x versicolor*), bear's breech (*Acanthus mollis*), bergenia (*Bergenia cordifolia*), bigroot geranium (*Geranium macrorrhizum*), false olive (*Phillyrea angustifolia*), fatsia (*Fatsia japonica*), firethorn (*Pyracantha*), hellebore (*Helleborus niger*), hydrangea (*Hydrangea macrophylla*), Japanese anemone (*Anemone x hybrida*), laurustinus (*Viburnum tinus*), meadow rue (*Thalictrum*), mourning widow (*Geranium phaeum*), periwinkle (*Vinca major*), pheasant-tailed grass (*Anemanthele lessoniana*), Portuguese laurel (*Prunus lusitanica*), skimmia (*Skimmia japonica*), shrubby hare's ear (*Bupleurum fruticosum*), wood spurge (*Euphorbia amygdaloides*)

Bulbs for a warmer garden

Mediterranean bulbs need a sunny spot, gritty, free-draining soil and should be mulched with grit. Leave them to die back and naturalise to bulk up into clumps.

Late spring: *Allium moly, Allium roseum, Anemone coronaria, Anemone blanda, Asphodelus lutea, Fritillaria acmopetala, Fritillaria persica, Iris attica, Muscari, Narcissus bulbocodium, Narcissus tazetta, Ornithogalum nutans, Tulipa saxatilis* and *Tulipa clusiana*

Summer to autumn: *Allium ampeloprasum, Allium nigrum, Allium atropurpureum, Allium sphhaerocephalon, Cyclamen hederifolium, Gladious communis, Iris foetidissima, Iris germanica, Iris pallida, Lilium candidum, Lilium martagon, Nectaroscordum siculum* and *Ornithogalum narbonense*

INDEX

SUPPORTERS

The publication of this book would not have been possible without the support of these two companies who backed our book idea from the start and understood exactly what we were trying to achieve.

Dalefoot Composts – the peat free champions

Dalefoot Composts has a unique 360 degree perspective on the 'peat in gardening' debate. Not only does this Lake District-based family firm make and champion the use of peat-free compost, it also restores damaged peat bogs across the UK for nature and environmental organisations. As peatlands erode or are harvested for horti-culture, carbon is released into the atmosphere accelerating global warming. Peatlands are a vital carbon store, formed over thousands of years. The peatland ecosystem is the most efficient carbon sink on the planet – it stores twice as much carbon as all of the earth's forests, however they only cover 3% of the earth's surface. Peatlands also play an important role in the hydrological cycle maintaining water quality, and helping in natural flood management by 'slowing the flow'. The company is passionate about saving peat and encouraging gardeners to switch to peat free. Its premium composts are made from sustainably-sourced bracken and Herdwick wool in the Lake District, so they are high in essential nutrients, feeding for up to two years and provide excellent moisture retention. You can read more here: www.dalefootcomposts.co.uk

First Tunnels

First Tunnels has been an industry leader for more than 20 years, providing polytunnels to domestic and commercial gardeners alike. Our passionate team of skilled professionals produces and supplies the highest quality polytunnels available in the UK. By extending the growing season for thousands of gardeners across the country, we take pride in helping people feed their families with fresh, nutritious food, and in boosting commercial yields of plant and flower crops. We work closely with schools, teaching children about the importance of healthy eating and bringing the class-room to the great outdoors. Based in the mill town of Altham, Lancashire, we are a big part of the local community. If you are ever in the area, feel free to swing on by to meet the team and see our manufacturing process in person. We do everything in house in order to guarantee quality and keep costs down for our valued customers. Those customers include NHS Trusts around the country, HM Prisons, schools, and other government organisations. We even supply gardening celebrities such as Alan Titchmarsh and Bob Flowerdew, as well as acclaimed chef Hugh Fearnley Whittingstall. You can read more here: www.firsttunnels.co.uk. We are proud to sponsor this important book